SUZANNE BARTLETT HACKENMILLER, MD

the outdoor adventurer's guide to

FOREST BATHING

D1556985

Using
SHINRIN-YOKU
to Hike, Bike,
Paddle, and Climb
Your Way to Health
and Happiness

FALCONGUIDES

GUILFORD, CONNECTICUT

To Joe—my forever adventure partner, my rock

FALCONGUIDES®

An imprint of The Rowman & Littlefield Publishing Group, Inc.
4501 Forbes Blvd., Ste. 200
Lanham, MD 20706
www.rowman.com

Falcon and FalconGuides are registered trademarks and Make Adventure Your Story is a trademark of The Rowman & Littlefield Publishing Group, Inc.

Distributed by NATIONAL BOOK NETWORK

Copyright © 2019 Suzanne Bartlett Hackenmiller, MD

Photos by author unless otherwise noted

British Library Cataloguing in Publication Information available

Library of Congress Cataloging-in-Publication Data available

ISBN 978-1-4930-4202-9 (paperback)
ISBN 978-1-4930-4203-6 (e-book)

∞™ The paper used in this publication meets the minimum requirements of American National Standard for Information Sciences—Permanence of Paper for Printed Library Materials, ANSI/NISO Z39.48-1992.

Printed in the United States of America

The authors and The Rowman & Littlefield Publishing Group, Inc. assume no liability for accidents happening to, or injuries sustained by, readers who engage in the activities described in this book.

Photo on previous page: Arches National Park, Moab, Utah

CONTENTS

INTRODUCTION

Outdoor adventure has been a source of great thrill, enjoyment, and accomplishment for me for many years. After my husband Dave passed away in 2012, both outdoor adventure and outdoor quiet time became my therapy. I had long found relief from a stressful medical practice in mountain biking, kayaking, scuba diving, and such, but it was the solace found in the contemplative time spent in nature that proved to be especially healing.

Jon Kabat-Zinn, the founder of Mindfulness-Based Stress Reduction, explains that "*mindfulness* means paying attention in a particular way: on purpose, in the present moment, and nonjudgmentally." As a formerly burned-out OB-GYN physician who studied and now practices integrative medicine, the concept of *mindfulness* was fascinating. For me, this *mindfulness* was most easily attained when I was outdoors in nature.

Outdoor adventure enthusiasts tend to use language such as "conquering," "shredding," and "bagging peaks." Unfortunately, I have witnessed that the very people one would expect to be stewards of outdoor spaces often destroy these spaces to the point that their activity is banned. I've seen many beautiful trails, for example, that now sadly sport No Mountain Biking signs. The world has also seen ski resorts

What is *Shinrin-Yoku* or Forest Bathing?

From *A Little Handbook of* Shinrin-Yoku by M. Amos Clifford

Forest Therapy, also known as "Shinrin-Yoku," refers to the practice of spending time in forested areas for the purpose of enhancing health, wellness, and happiness. The practice follows the general principle that it is beneficial to spend time bathing in the atmosphere of the forest. The Japanese words translate into English as "Forest Bathing." Although we are inspired by the Japanese practice, our use of the terms Forest Therapy and Shinrin-Yoku do not mean a specifically Japanese practice. We mean spending time in nature in a way that invites healing interactions. There is a long tradition of this in cultures throughout the world. It's not just about healing people; it includes healing for the forest (or river, or desert, or whatever environment you are in).

There are an infinite number of healing activities that can be incorporated into a walk in a forest or any other natural area. An activity is likely to be healing when it makes room for listening, for quiet and accepting presence, and for inquiry through all eight of the sensory modes we possess.

This view of healing interactions implies some baseline requirements for Shinrin-Yoku and Forest Therapy:

1. There is a specific intention to connect with nature in a healing way. This requires mindfully moving through the landscape in ways that cultivate presence, opening all the senses, and actively communicating with the land.

2. It is not something to rush through. Shinrin-Yoku walks are not undertaken with the primary goal of physical exercise. We prefer to avoid the term "hiking" because of its implications of physical exertion. As taught by the Association, Shinrin-Yoku walks are typically a mile or less and range in duration from two to four hours.

3. Healing interactions require giving generously of our attention. We encourage mindfulness through an evolving series of suggested invitations. Each invitation is crafted to help participants slow down and open our senses. As we do this we begin to perceive more deeply the nuances of the constant stream of communications rampant in any natural setting. We learn to let the land and its messages penetrate into our minds and hearts more deeply.

4. It's not a one-time event. Developing a meaningful relationship with nature occurs over time, and is deepened by returning again and again throughout the natural cycles of the seasons. Like yoga, meditation, prayer, working out, and many other worthy endeavors, Shinrin-Yoku is a practice. And because it is a practice, it is best to learn it from a qualified guide.

5. It's not just about taking walks in the forest. The walks are important, but there are other core routines that we can do that will help in our deepening relationship with nature, and in the exchange of health benefits between humans and the more-than-human-world. We often incorporate some of these practices in our guided Shinrin-Yoku walks, particularly the practices of sit spot, place tending, and cross-species communication.

These five elements together provide a framework for the practice of Forest Therapy. *A Little Handbook of* Shinrin-Yoku, M. Amos Clifford, 2013, p. 7–8.

with huge carbon footprints that threaten the very future of snow. Bringing mindfulness practices to outdoor enthusiasts is an ideal way to address this. After contemplating gratitude for nature, or slowing down long enough to absorb the awe of one's surroundings, it becomes impossible to recklessly damage these spaces. I have witnessed this revelation among outdoor enthusiasts, and it is most definitely profound.

Currently there is a mindfulness movement encouraged by sports psychologists and adopted by many competitive adventure athletes, where practices such as meditation and guided imagery are incorporated into training regimens. Jamie Anderson, United States snowboarding gold medalist, spoke publicly about her mindfulness practices, as well as a number of other integrative approaches she employs. I believe this is the future of competitive sports.

In 2014 I discovered *shinrin-yoku*, or Japanese forest bathing. I was intrigued and determined to learn more. I connected with Amos

Clifford, founder and CEO of the international Association of Nature and Forest Therapy (ANFT). Fast-forward to today, when I guide groups and individuals in *shinrin-yoku* and find it to be some of the most effective medicine in my tool bag. I am now the medical director of ANFT, a role I am most passionate about. My husband, Joe, and I lead workshops combining outdoor adventure and forest bathing.

While the term "forest bathing" sounds as if it would require a forest, in reality this practice can be done in any outdoor setting. One thing that sets forest bathing apart from mindfulness, in its truest sense of the word, is that in mindfulness practices, the object is to remove oneself from emotion and reaction to one's surroundings. In forest bathing, however, there is a celebration of the experience of awe and wonder during time spent in nature.

The Outdoor Adventurer's Guide to Forest Bathing serves to marry these two things that I love, with the purpose of helping readers become more mindful as they engage in outdoor adventure. This serves to improve the health and well-being of the individuals themselves, while also serving to create greater awareness and a sense of oneness with our natural spaces. In a time where over 300 million people are visiting natural parks per year, there has never been a more timely need for this movement in order to protect our natural treasures.

The Standard Sequence of Forest Bathing

The practice of *shinrin-yoku*, or Japanese forest bathing, as it is used in the United States and developed by Amos Clifford, involves following what is known as the "Standard Sequence." This means that certain elements are employed in each and every guided forest bathing or forest therapy walk. The Standard Sequence allows for a number of things to be true: (1) There is standardization among ANFT-certified guides, worldwide, and standardization among the types of experience a participant may expect to have on a guided walk. (2) The Standard Sequence is designed to optimally take the participant from the everyday cognitive, conscious, monkey-mind state to a liminal, dreamlike, subconscious state, and then ultimately back to the everyday, conscious (hopefully less monkey-mind) state by the conclusion of the walk. (3) Standardization across forest bathing walks allows for this practice to be replicable, and therefore amenable to scientific research.

A guided forest bathing walk involves the use of "invitations" and the use of "council," two terms that will be further clarified. Guides "invite" participants to consider taking nature in through the various senses, via a number of specific approaches. As the term implies, these approaches are not mandatory—they are merely invitations. These invitations are created with a goal of bringing people to the edge of their comfort zone, in order to achieve the aforementioned "liminal state." It is, of course, crucial to any lasting healing modality to push the edges of our comfort zone, as this is where the magic invariably happens.

Webster's dictionary defines *council* as "an assembly or meeting for consultation, advice, or discussion." In forest bathing, it is customary for the participant(s) and the guide to come together following each invitation to simply share what they may have noticed during the invitation. This may be a one-word noticing, or it may be a more involved sharing of one's experience. It is believed that this act of sharing helps to solidify the experience in one's body and mind and serves to amplify its healing effects. Amos Clifford teaches that sharing in council is much like sharing a dream in an effort to commit it to memory. Journaling

after forest bathing has a similar effect, much like keeping a dream journal, and is a highly recommended component of forest bathing.

A key component to forest bathing is the concept of the "edge." A goal of the forest therapy guide is to bring each participant to the edge of his or her comfort zone. This comfort zone is different for each and every person. For one forest bather, it may be an edge to take his or her shoes off or to physically come in contact with a tree. For another, it may be an edge to simply stand with eyes closed during the Pleasures of Presence. The recommendation is to simply observe that edge, attempting not to judge or fear it, recognizing that everyone experiences it in different ways. It is believed that personal growth happens when we encounter the limits of our comfort zone, whether physically (such as in the practice of adventurous sport) or emotionally, mentally, or spiritually, as commonly occurs during the practice of forest bathing. As readers practice the invitations in this book, it is hoped that the "edge" will be encountered and that growth will occur in a variety of ways.

The first invitation in the Standard Sequence is called the "Pleasures of Presence." It has also been referred to as "Embodied Awareness," because it is an invitation that serves to systematically bring the natural surroundings into the physical body via the senses of sound, touch, smell, taste, and sight. Participants typically take part in the Standard Sequence with eyes closed as the guide brings awareness to their surroundings in a stepwise fashion. The Pleasures of Presence is followed by council, where participants are invited (but not required) to share what they noticed during the invitation.

The Standard Sequence next invites participants to notice "What's in Motion." This can be done while standing or sitting still, or while walking. Often when hiking or walking along a trail, people will find that they remain stuck with their head engrossed in the issues of the day, never moving their eyes or awareness much beyond their footsteps. Upon the conclusion of the hike, the ruminations are still there, stuck in the mind, unchanged. What if turning one's attention to something as simple as noticing what is in motion could provide some much-needed clarity and space for answers to arise? During "What's in Motion?" participants are invited to walk very slowly (or stop in one place if they wish), paying particular attention to noticing what is visibly in motion. If and when the mind wanders or is distracted by something else, participants are encouraged to gently return their attention to noticing what is in motion. Ten to twenty minutes is the recommended duration of noticing what is in motion. Sharing in council is invited.

There is an infinite number of invitations that a guide will then include in a forest bathing walk. These may be one of the many "tried-and-true" invitations often used in ANFT guide training, or they may be invented specifically for a particular group, activity, season, or event. Anyone can create forest therapy invitations! Each invitation is followed by some form of council. Sometimes council involves the full group, sometimes it is done in pairs or small groups. There is a variety of different forms of council that a guide may choose to employ.

"Sit Spot" is an invitation that is traditionally recommended toward the culmination of a forest bathing walk. This invitation is just as it sounds, an invitation to simply sit . . . for twenty minutes. Besides the initial shock in our fast-paced society of being invited to simply *sit*, this invitation often serves as an opportunity for profound bonding with nature. During Sit Spot, there is no agenda. There is no expectation to meditate, pray, chant, strike a yoga pose, journal, or do anything other than sit in silence surrounded by nature. This practice may be done in the most modest of natural surroundings, by the way, and numerous forest therapy guides around the globe have been known to perform this practice on porches and balconies in urban settings, with little more than a potted plant or a single tree. During the course of a twenty-minute Sit Spot, it is said that "something happens" with the beings in the more-than-human world. The insects, animals, and birds become less threatened by our presence, and connection simply happens. Following the Sit Spot invitation, council and/or journaling is encouraged.

In keeping with the inspiration of Japanese tradition, the final invitation of *shinrin-yoku* is the tea ceremony. In forests where foraging is permitted and where chemical pesticides and herbicides are not used, it is customary for the forest therapy guide to choose an edible local plant

from which to prepare tea. It is absolutely imperative—and this cannot be overemphasized—that the tea ceremony be led by a qualified guide, as poisonous plants do exist and potential adverse effects may occur from ingesting plants with potential medicinal properties.

It has been my privilege to study herbal medicine with one of the foremost experts in the field, Dr. Tieraona Low Dog, so I love nothing more than sharing the ancient healing wisdom of our local plants with the people who come on my walks. Also, during the tea ceremony, I often will share some of the exciting scientific studies about nature and its effects on health. It is this return to our cognitive, conscious way of thinking that is known as the "Threshold of Incorporation" in the Standard Sequence.

Mountain bikes and lupines, Lutsen, Minnesota

Please note that the terms *shinrin-yoku*, forest bathing, and forest therapy are used interchangeably in this book.

What Is Included in This Book?

This guidebook includes the activities of hiking, paddling, mountain biking, rock climbing, cross-country skiing, and trail running. The chapters include examples of forest bathing "invitations" that may be used before, during, or after taking part in each particular form of outdoor adventure.

Although many elite athletes may not be familiar with the terms "forest bathing" or *shinrin-yoku*, conversations with these individuals suggest that many of them employ various mindful techniques in the practice of their sport. In fact, many of these mindful techniques involve the absorption of natural surroundings in ways that very much mimic the practice of forest bathing. It is readily apparent that the calming properties of nature are a component of many athletes' success. The chapters of this book contain conversations and interviews with some elite athletes on the topic of nature and mindfulness as it pertains to their proficiency in their sport.

This guidebook also includes sidebars that incorporate information on related topics, such as:

- Research regarding nature and wellness
- Information on plant wisdom and herbal medicine
- Neurodiversity and special populations

Finally, this guidebook offers an acknowledgment of the ancestral inhabitants of our natural spaces, often referred to as "public land." Much injustice has been done to indigenous people around the world, and there is a component of forest bathing that not only recognizes the ancestral history of the land, but also acknowledges historical wrongdoings. A simple way to honor the Native population is to first learn the indigenous name of the land upon which you are standing. As part of your practice, you might include a statement such as, "I acknowledge that we are standing upon the traditional lands of the Iowa, the Sauk, the Meskwaki, and the Sioux. I would like to thank them for their stewardship of the land." Information and an interactive map of ancestral lands are available on the Native Land app at www.native-land.ca.

Who Should Read This Book and Why?

This guidebook is unique in that it unites the elements of *adventure* in nature and *mindfulness* in nature. In my interactions with people,

Loess Hills, western Iowa

I recognize that many of us are seeking *experience* and seeking *wellness* like never before.

I believe this guidebook provides healing and wellness to those who explore its modalities. As John Muir said, "In every walk with nature one receives far more than he seeks." I believe, too, that as a mindfulness practice, *shinrin-yoku* has potential to improve the performance of athletes. This guidebook not only combines adventure, mindfulness, and herbal medicine, but also provides scientific research findings that support the benefits of time spent in nature and mindfulness in nature.

Finally, I believe this guidebook is empowering at an eco-consciousness level; it creates an awareness and oneness, if you will, with nature that will serve to protect our natural treasures. The forest heals us, which, in turn, heals the forest.

Whether you are a novice outdoor adventurer or an elite athlete, this guidebook is for you. It is applicable for those guiding groups of children and adults in recreational, camp, and educational settings. Those working with special populations, such as cancer survivors, individuals on the autism spectrum, and people with mental conditions such as depression, anxiety, insomnia, and post-traumatic stress disorder (PTSD), are invited to use this book for guidance.

How to Use This Book

It is my hope that outdoor enthusiasts will find that this guide forever changes the way they interact with nature. It is my hope that greater connections between people and the more-than-human world will serve to protect our outdoor spaces for generations to come.

If you share a love for all the activities outlined in this book, I hope you will read it cover to cover. If just one or two of these activities are your passion, I hope the chapters on those topics add greater meaning and enjoyment to your adventures.

If you have considered trying one of these activities for the first time, perhaps the elements of forest bathing will help draw you in. If you are an accomplished athlete, my hope is that these practices will enhance your experience and your abilities.

When the "aha" moments happen, I hope you will share your discoveries with me. After all, it is my belief that the revelations of the collective council can heal us all and can heal the planet. They certainly heal the healer.

HIKING

I have had the good fortune of some life-changing day hikes in my life: to the top of an active volcano in Tanna, Vanuatu; to the top of Half Dome in Yosemite National Park; to the peninsula of Kalaupapa in Molokai, Hawaii; among others. But the most memorable hike was foreshadowed by a dream, and its subsequent events and synchronicities ultimately led to my work in nature and forest therapy—a story for another book, another day. The hike was at Yosemite Falls, North America's tallest waterfall, and I commissioned my two children, John and Elise, to join me. At eleven and thirteen years old, it was more adventure than they may have anticipated or hoped for . . . but they did it.

After several hours of steep climbing and switchbacks, John tripped and scraped his knee. At that point, he was mentally and physically done—but I knew we couldn't retreat just yet. As I knelt next to him rendering first aid and a pep talk, the guide of a group of hikers approached us and asked if we were OK. I will admit that we had been trying to stay ahead of this chatty group for hours, so I was a little annoyed that they had caught up. But then the guide said, "If you're interested, we're going to take a little-known route across these rocks and get back behind the upper falls. You're welcome to join us." My eyes may have popped out of my head.

We joined the group, climbing over huge boulders, until we were in a cavern behind the enormous falls. It was breathtaking and surreal. After the guided hiking group finished their photo ops, they took off. We thanked the guide and decided to spend a bit more time. For the next hour or so my kids and I remained, completely alone, suspended in time and place, playing, picnicking, and lying on enormous boulders in the sun, with the spray of Yosemite Falls misting down upon us. Our Yosemite Falls hike is one that I hope my kids will never forget. For me, not only was the hike memorable, but it also confirmed my calling to share with others the healing energy of outdoor adventure and the powerful medicine of nature.

Trail Stewardship

The American Hiking Society (AHS) "envisions a world where every American has permanent access to a hiking trail," according to its website (www.americanhiking.org). The organization preserves trails "by facilitating trail maintenance, protecting natural spaces by advocating, and promoting hiking by inspiring and equipping people to get out on the trail." At the time of this writing, the AHS website boasts having mobilized over 558,000 trail volunteers and facilitated over 41,000 miles of trail maintenance and construction, and that their volunteers have contributed over $100 million in volunteer labor to the 200,000-plus miles of trails that cover the United States. Individuals may join the organization on weeklong "Volunteer Vacations" across the United States and its territories, where they backpack and day hike in exciting destinations building and maintaining trails.

Today, there are a number of programs in addition to the AHS that invite people from all walks of life to get outdoors and enjoy hiking,

walking, and other forms of physical activity. I have been privileged to meet and work with the founders of a number of these programs. Thanks to Christian Beckwith, founder of the organization SHIFT (www.shiftjh.org), many of these leaders were recognized and brought together with hopes for future collaboration at a conference in Jackson Hole, Wyoming, in the fall of 2018. Some of these organizations are described in the paragraphs and chapters that follow.

One cannot imagine too many things that are better for kids than getting outdoors, and more and more research is supporting this. Organizations such as Park Rx America, Kids in Parks, and Free Forest School are making it easier for parents to find parks and trails all over the United States and to connect with other families.

Park Rx America was founded by Dr. Robert Zarr, a pediatrician in Washington, DC, with the goal of getting kids outdoors, moving and playing. With their new online platform, doctors across the United States can locate a park close to where their patients live and prescribe a specific activity that the patient enjoys, along with "dose and frequency" of their prescription. Patients can even report back to their doctor via technology. Learn more at www.parkrxamerica.org.

A great way to find kid-friendly trails is to explore the Kids in Parks program, which is under the direction of Jason Urroz. As described on its website, "Kids in Parks is an expanding network of family-friendly outdoor adventures called TRACK Trails. Each TRACK Trail features self-guided brochures and signs that turn your visit into a fun and exciting outdoors experience. Best of all, you can earn PRIZES for tracking your adventures!" Find trails and more information at www .kidsinparks.com.

Anna Sharratt founded the program Free Forest School. Its mission statement sums it up: "Free Forest School ignites children's innate capacity to learn through unstructured play in nature, fostering healthy development and nurturing the next generation of creative thinkers, collaborative leaders and environmental stewards." Grassroots chapters have sprung up around the globe, connected by social media, and can be found at www.freeforestschool.org.

There is a movement among leaders of minority groups to encourage time spent in nature among people of color. I have been most impressed by the initiatives Corazón Latino, One Common Unity, and Wings of America.

Founded by Felipe Benítez, Corazón Latino "catalyzes conceptualization, design, and implementation of culturally relevant campaigns to inform, empower, and mobilize diverse communities around environmental, conservation, education, civic engagement, social justice and health issues through strategic communications and grassroots mobilization tools." They work to engage Latino youth in outdoor activities

The Science of Nature: A Mental Boost!

Did you know that a 2008 study showed that participants' memory and attention span improved by 20 percent after just one hour walking and interacting in nature? The best part is that the study found that the benefit still occurred whether or not the participants enjoyed the walk, due to factors like weather, mosquitoes, etc. (Berman et al. 2008). So, the next time you drag your whining children outdoors on a hike in the woods, remember this study and the mental and cognitive benefits you are providing them!

and also aid and support disaster relief and reconstruction work, in areas such as hurricane-devastated Puerto Rico, for a more resilient and sustainable future. This and more information about Corazón Latino is available on the website www.corazonlatino.us.

One Common Unity was started by the charismatic leader Hawah Kasat, with the mission of breaking cycles of violence and building compassionate, healthy communities through the transformative power of music, arts, and peace education. The award-winning documentary *Fly by Light* shares the intimate journey of the program's at-risk youth who are taken on a transformative retreat, away from the stressors of the city, and into nature. For more information, visit www .onecommonunity.org.

Since 1988, Wings of America has brought about social and environmental change through running programs, currently with running camps for Native American youth in Arizona, New Mexico, Oklahoma, New York, and South Dakota. "Inspired by the cultural, spiritual and competitive legacy of Native runners, Wings empowers Native youth and their families," according to its website. In 2018, Wings of America's executive director, Dustin Martin, worked with other organizations to coordinate the event "Sacred Strides for Healing," where several Native tribes, previously at odds with each other, have come together for the purpose of creating awareness, honoring, and reclaiming the Bears Ears National Monument in southern Utah. Runners from tribes in Arizona, Utah, and Colorado crossed nearly 800 miles to converge at the ancestral lands of Bears Ears. This land was designated a national monument by President Obama in 2016, only to have that designation overturned by President Trump in 2017, paving the way for extraction and exploitation of the region. For more information about this history, these initiatives, and the work of Wings of America, visit www.wingsofamerica.org.

Neurodiversity/Special Populations and Forest Bathing

As a mother of a child with autism, some of the most rewarding work I have done has been in autism advocacy. I have also been asked to share forest bathing, at times, with neurodiverse populations. On one occasion, I had the privilege to guide a group of adults with intellectual disabilities at a self-advocacy conference held at a lakeside resort. In this instance, a number of participants used wheelchairs, which initially seemed like an insurmountable challenge. It turned out that I was able to guide the group along a paved sidewalk that on one side was lined with wildflowers and on the other had an organic vegetable garden. We then proceeded toward a lawn filled with mature trees, which even the wheelchairs were able to reach. It was one of my first realizations that forest bathing is truly accessible to everyone.

I have also led groups of individuals with autism in forest bathing. As sensory overload is often a challenge for people with autism spectrum disorders (ASD), to me it seems like forest bathing might be an excellent fit. My friend Tyler Leech is an adult who identifies as having autism, and has been a big proponent of forest bathing. He also happens to be a "barefooter" who has fully embraced the concept of grounding in nature. I asked Tyler if I could share the statement on his Barefoot Autism Challenge Facebook page, and he enthusiastically agreed:

"People with autism may experience different sensory experiences or have trouble with proprioception. They may have a limited ability to connect with themselves because they cannot connect with the world around them when they are shod. For many people with autism, walking barefoot helps calm down their nerves and lessens their stress while the varying textures awaken their world. Those with autism appear to be more alert and in tune with their surroundings while they are barefoot.

"Hi, my name is Tyler. I have autism. I want to challenge you. Whether you have autism or not, I want you to put yourself in the

"shoes" of someone with autism—or rather take them off—and take part in the Barefoot Autism Challenge. Go to a location like a park, a trail, a sidewalk, the beach, etc., and take the challenge by removing your shoes and submersing yourself in your environment. Feel the earth. Connect with it, and connect with yourself. Then post a picture or video on social media and at the Barefoot Autism Challenge's Facebook page at www.facebook.com/BarefootAutism Challenge/. Most importantly, share what advocating for someone with autism means to you. Challenge as many friends as you like using #barefootautismchallenge."

Medical experts are beginning to acknowledge that a sense of community is one of the critical pillars of health. In fact, the "Blue Zones" of the world—the places where people have been found to live the longest, healthiest lives—are all areas where importance is placed on spending time with others. These places all have a common thread that involves families and friends sharing meals together, exercising together, and often living together. Sadly, the fast-paced lifestyles and technological advances in many developed countries has meant a loss of that sense of community. There are a number of organizations that have recognized the importance of being with others, two of which are highlighted below.

Since 2013 I have enjoyed getting outdoors with patients, simply walking and talking about wellness, with the program "Walk with a Doc," founded by Dr. David Sabgir, a cardiologist in Columbus, Ohio. This program, founded in 2005, was prompted by Dr. Sabgir's difficulties in motivating his patients to engage in physical activity. He invited them to join him for a walk in the park one Saturday morning, and was shocked when over a hundred people showed up. Now there are chapters all over the world. Find one near you at www.walkwithadoc.org.

Individuals with disabilities and those with various medical conditions are able to find their tribe and the necessary accommodations through a number of organizations. The mission of Dream Adaptive Recreation, Inc., is to enhance the quality of life of individuals with disabilities by providing year-round outdoor adaptive recreational opportunities. DREAM, which stands for Disabled Recreation Environmental Access Movement, offers programming for individuals with visual impairments, amputations, spinal cord injuries, multiple sclerosis, head injuries, cerebral palsy, and other neuromuscular/orthopedic conditions, along with autism and related intellectual disabilities. Its

website is www.dreamadaptive.org. Additional adaptive nature and recreation programs can be found through a quick online search.

Whether walking in a park, playing outdoors in nature, finding community, or finding solitude, it is increasingly apparent that time spent in nature is good for us. Finding what works for each of us is certainly (pun intended) the first step.

Mindfulness in Hiking

Many people report feeling a sense of mental clarity after hiking in nature. In fact, a study of proofreading proficiency compared participants who backpacked in the wilderness, those who backpacked in an urban setting, and those who had no backpacking trip at all. It

found that the participants who backpacked in nature had statistically significant improvement in their ability to proofread written passages. Those who backpacked in the urban setting showed no improvement whatsoever and were statistically the same as those who stayed home (Hartig et al. 1991, 2003).

Walking meditation is a practice that can be used anywhere, be it a labyrinth, a nature trail, or even indoors. Jon Kabat-Zinn, the founder of Mindfulness-Based Stress Reduction, describes it as "not about getting somewhere on foot. Instead, you are being with each step, fully here, where you actually are. You are not trying to get anywhere, even to the next step. There is no arriving, other than continually arriving in the present moment" (Kabat-Zinn 2018). The idea is to keep one's gaze soft, noticing the intricacies of each step, from the movements involved in elevating each foot slowly, noticing the movement in every joint and the sensation of the foot leaving and re-touching the ground, noticing the temperature of the air and the sounds and smells of the surroundings. Typically, it is recommended that steps be counted such that ten or so steps are taken before the meditator stops, takes some slow, cleansing breaths, and turns around to repeat the same number of steps in the opposite direction. This is done back and forth for a predetermined number of times.

For some, walking meditation may be awkward. It can be difficult to keep the mind from wandering, and may seem unnatural. The goal of detachment from the awe and wonder of one's natural surroundings may also seem disappointing. Forest bathing employs a combination of some of the features of mindfulness—losing oneself in the moment, for example—but celebrates the feeling of awe and wonder.

FOREST BATHING/SHINRIN-YOKU AND HIKING

INVITATIONS BEFORE HIKING
Pleasures of Presence

It is easy (and fairly common) to spend an entire hike rarely looking up from the trail. This is a common revelation that participants often report after their first experience with forest bathing. A great way to modify this habit is to precede a hike with the "Pleasures of Presence" invitation.

Invitation: Start by surveying your surroundings and searching for a leaf, pinecone, flower, or other plant-related artifact. Pick up an item that appeals to you. For the purposes of this description, it will be a pinecone. You may sit or stand for this invitation.

I had the pleasure of visiting with Liz Thomas, author of *Long Trails: Mastering the Art of the Thru-Hike*. A kindred spirit in the realm of finding mindfulness in nature, Thomas is among the most experienced female hikers in the United States and is known for backpacking light, fast, and solo. The bio on her website (www.eathomas.com) states, "In 2011, she broke the women's unsupported speed record on the 2,181-mile long Appalachian Trail, besting the previous record by almost a week. She has completed the Triple Crown of Hiking—the Appalachian Trail, the 2,650-mile Pacific Crest Trail, and the 3,100-mile Continental Divide Trail—and has backpacked over 15,000 miles across the United States on 16 long distance hikes, including the pioneering traverse of the Chinook Trail across the Columbia River Gorge and the pioneering traverse of the Wasatch Range, which she did solo."

Thomas holds a master's degree in environmental science from the Yale School of Forestry and Environmental Studies as well as the prestigious Doris Duke Conservation Fellowship "for her research on long distance hiking trails, conservation, and trail town communities—a project she is applying in her work with the trail non-profit Continental Divide Trail Coalition," her bio goes on to say. She is vice president of the American Long-Distance Hiking Association–West, one of four ambassadors for the American Hiking Society, and the instructor for *Backpacker Magazine*'s first-ever "Introduction to Thru-Hiking" course. She is also a national speaker and has been featured in numerous well-known publications.

In a post on her blog titled "Why Adrenaline Junkies Get Bored Hiking," Thomas writes, "There is simple peace to be had in sitting in nature. Walking slowly in nature. Letting nature dictate you and not the other way around." She goes on to say, "Each plant, lichen, moss, rock, leaf, caterpillar, flower, and footstep becomes something to relish."

The blog proceeds to share additional words of wisdom. "On a long-distance hike, thinking ahead to Canada when you're standing at the

Mexican border is way too overwhelming," she writes. "There is peace to be had by not thinking too much farther ahead. By living in the present."

I asked Thomas in what way she finds nature to be healing. She replied, "I think that humans evolved to spend much more time in nature than we do. And so, I think my whole community of thru-hikers revolves their life around trying to make it work that they can spend two, four, six months every year doing it, because it's almost like this migration. It's something that comes from deep within that *has* to happen. At least within our community, it's kind of a given that it's their call, that it's something deep in our gut, deep in our soul."

With her work in environmental studies, I asked Thomas if she thinks that spending time outdoors makes people more environmentally conscious. "*For sure*," she said. "Definitely, for sure. My big thing is conservation, specifically protecting lands from development. . . . And I think when people spend time, personally, in a forest walking or just taking it in, there's a sort of appreciation and understanding of why it's important that these places exist, that they exist close to where people live." Thomas went on to comment, "It's not about just being human-centric, but starting to appreciate all the other creatures that we share the earth with."

Follow Liz on Instagram at @lizthomashiking.

Begin by closing your eyes once you are in a comfortable position. With your eyes closed, hold your pinecone in one hand and gently pass if from one hand to the next. What do you notice about the weight of the pinecone? What about the size of it? Does it fit in the palm of one or both hands, or is it larger than your hands? If you squeeze the pinecone, what does that feel like? Does it feel like it would crush between your hands, or does it feel strong and uncrushable? Do parts of it move when you squeeze it? What does the texture of the pinecone feel like? Is it rough or smooth? Is it prickly? Does the texture surprise you at all? Does it feel gritty or dirty? What is the temperature of the pinecone? Is it warmer or colder than your hands? Does it feel dry, or does it feel as if it contains moisture? If you hold the pinecone up to your cheek, how does it feel against your face? What else do you notice about the way the pinecone feels?

Next, hold your pinecone up to your nose and smell it. What does it smell like? Does it smell the way you expected it to? Does it remind you of anything? Does it bring back any memories? Do all sides of the pinecone share the same scent? Do you feel like tasting it with the tip of your tongue? If so, try it!

Now bring the pinecone up to your ear. Move it between your palm and fingers or between two hands while you listen to the sound that the movement creates. Does the sound seem hollow or dense? Is the pitch high or low? How does this change if you tap or run your fingers across different parts of the pinecone? If you don't move it at all and just listen to your pinecone, is there any sound at all?

Finally, return your pinecone in front of your chest and hold it in one or both hands, still with eyes closed. Take a moment to revisit all of the senses you just took in and imagine that you have never seen this object before. Take a moment to imagine what it would be like to

have no idea what this thing in your hands is. Give yourself a moment or two and then go ahead and open your eyes. Visually absorb what you are seeing with brand-new eyes. Notice the dark areas, the light areas, whether your pinecone is shiny or dull-looking. Notice the color or colors as if for the very first time. Notice the fractals or repeating patterns in your pinecone and turn it over and around to see how these patterns change. Have you ever noticed this before?

Share what you noticed with any other individuals with whom you are appreciating the Pleasures of Presence, or take a moment to journal about what you noticed. Even a few notes will help to solidify the experience in your memory.

INVITATIONS DURING HIKING
Pleasures of Presence

You may also decide to incorporate the Pleasures of Presence into your hike after you start walking. Whether you repeat this invitation at the beginning of the hike or later on, many people find it to dramatically alter their experience.

Invitation: As you hike, choose one of the senses. You may decide to set an amount of time (five, ten, or twenty minutes, for example) to devote to focusing on each sense as you walk.

Perhaps you will start with your sense of smell. Take some slow, deep breaths in through your nose as you walk down the trail. What is the first scent you notice? Can you identify it? What do you notice about that scent, and does it trigger any memories? As you walk, notice whether you continue to smell the same scent that originally caught your attention or whether it has been replaced with new scents. While focusing on your sense of smell, you may be moved to stop and smell a particular plant, flower, or the bark of a tree. Close your eyes and take it in fully. You may even decide to scoop up some soil or forest floor detritus—the shed vegetative parts (leaves, bark, tree branches) that exist above the soil in various stages of decomposition—and take a whiff.* What do you notice when you smell the soil or forest floor? How does it make you feel? You can spend a great deal of time—even an entire hike—simply noticing the smells of nature that surround you.

Complete the same process using the other senses, perhaps for a set period of time, while you hike. What do you hear? Can you isolate sounds from different directions or distances? What is the highest-pitch sound you can hear? The lowest? If you stop walking, is there complete silence or is there a background noise? How do the sounds of your footsteps interact with the sounds of nature? Are there rhythmic sounds? Are there "conversations" between animals, birds, and insects? What else do you hear from the more-than-human world?

What do you see? Focus on different visual findings as you walk. Do you notice different shades of green? Of brown? What other colors do you notice? Do you notice patterns?

After the Pleasures of Presence, what do you notice about your awareness as you continue to hike?

What's in Motion?

The invitation "What's in Motion?" is perfectly suited to hiking since, after all, forest bathing typically is done while walking. The difference is that most people hike at a faster pace than is used in forest bathing.

---

*A word of caution: A rare, but potentially dangerous, medical condition called hantavirus pulmonary syndrome (HPS) can be transmitted by inhaling airborne droplets of rodent urine, droppings, or nesting materials that contain the hantavirus. Forests and fields, as well as dilapidated buildings, barns, and outbuildings, are common areas where rodents are found. Care should be taken not to stir up soil that may have been inhabited by rodents, and to avoid touching and breathing in any potentially contaminated material.

Forest bathing at Prairiewoods Retreat Center, Hiawatha, Iowa

Invitation: As you hike, bring your awareness to noticing what is visibly in motion. Doing so will naturally widen your gaze beyond the space immediately ahead of your feet. Plan to spend a set period of time—perhaps even set a timer on your watch or phone—of ten to twenty minutes for this invitation. As you walk, just notice what is moving in your surroundings. If you wish to stop and investigate the movement of a small plant or insect, allow yourself to do so. If and when your attention is distracted by a sound or another person or thing, just remember to nonjudgmentally return your awareness to noticing what is in motion. When you are done, share your findings with another person or take a moment to reflect upon what you noticed.

Thresholds of Connection

The Cambridge English dictionary defines a threshold as a "starting point" or an "entrance." It goes on to define it as "the level or point at which you start to experience something, or at which something starts to happen or change." During a hike, it can be interesting to pay attention to various types of thresholds as you walk on a trail through a forest or other natural setting.

Invitation: While hiking, set the intention that you are going to be on the lookout for various types of thresholds for a specific period of time, say twenty minutes. These thresholds may involve any of the sensory processes, and may even involve your intuition. Examples include noticing the moment at which any of the following occur: a temperature change; a change in light or darkness; a change in vegetation; a change in trail composition; walking through or over something, such as a natural arch; a change in ambient sound or noise; a change in the moisture content of the air; a change in behavior of wildlife in your midst. You may even notice a threshold where you intuitively realize you are in harm's way. What other thresholds do you notice? If you spend some time at these various thresholds of connection, what do you notice?

Finding Life in Death and Decay

Outdoor environments—forests, deserts, aquatic ecosystems—are continuous cycles of life and death, where dying plant and animal material feeds other living beings in a perfectly orchestrated circle of life. It is easy to overlook signs of death and decay; we seem hardwired to try to avoid them.

Invitation: As you hike, you are invited to notice and seek out signs of death and decay. You may notice a downed tree or tree branch and take a closer look. Use all of your senses. Perhaps you notice (or smell!) a dead animal, and instead of running the other way, go ahead and take a quick look. What do you see? As you walk, you might decide to pick up some leaves and woody debris from the forest floor. What do you notice within this material? What do you notice on the bare ground when you brush this debris aside? Investigate mushrooms and fungi when you come across them. Do you notice leaves that have holes in them? What do you think is happening there? How does it make you feel to take notice of death and decay in nature? What emotions arise? Is there a message for you in this process?

Hero's Journey

Countless stories, movies, tales, and fables are based on the "Hero's Journey," a template whereby a hero strikes out on an adventure, wins a victory amid some form of crisis, and then returns home changed or transformed. The Hero's Journey, as described by the scholar Joseph Campbell and others, has been used therapeutically in a number of contexts. A hiking trail can be symbolic of a miniature Hero's Journey.

Invitation: Imagine, as you hike, that you are setting out on a Hero's Journey. Perhaps you will need to protect yourself with some armor, a shield, or a "weapon" such as a stick. Muster up some childhood imagination as you set out on your adventure. You may not encounter an actual physical crisis (hopefully!), but instead simply notice what obstacles arise on your trail. These may be such things as rocks and roots along the trail, muddy areas, water crossings, nuisance insects, or even things like temperature extremes. Simply take note of these obstacles and your response to them.

Continue on in this way for a time (or maybe for your entire hike), and when you feel you have completed your Hero's Journey, ask yourself what you are noticing about your emotions. Does it remind you of anything or trigger a memory? Is there a message for you in this experience? Did your hero emerge transformed?

Hug a Tree

Admittedly, the concept of forest bathing is fairly analogous to "tree hugging." But have you ever tried it?

Invitation: Take a look around at the trees that are nearby and see if a particular tree seems to catch your attention. Walk over to that tree and just stand next to it for a moment. Sometimes, in forest bathing, we invite our participants to introduce themselves to a tree. You may do that, or you may simply step closer and put your hands on the tree. Spend at least ten minutes in physical contact with the tree, in some manner. Options include touching the tree with your hands, sitting or standing with your back to the tree, or wrapping your arms around it in full embrace. Whatever you choose, just stay there and notice what it feels like to hug a tree. What do you notice about the temperature, texture, strength, and perhaps even vibrations from within the tree? What is it like to officially qualify as a tree hugger?

Treasure Hunt

Who doesn't enjoy a treasure hunt? There are variations on this theme—the sky's the limit!

Invitation: Invite yourself to search for natural treasures. As you hike, allow curiosity to dominate your thoughts. If something catches your eye, investigate it. If it is attached or growing, allow yourself to take some time to explore the object and ask yourself why it caught your eye. If the item is unattached/not growing, and is small enough (and safe) to pick up, go ahead and pick it up and, again, ask yourself what drew you to the item. Use common sense, of course, when touching and gathering items in nature. Continue on, allowing your attention to be drawn toward whatever you are called to notice. You may even ask yourself if the items you notice in any way serve as a metaphor for something in your life. I like to ask myself "How is *this* like *that*?" In other words, how is this thing that caught my attention (e.g., a feather stuck in a cactus) like an emotion or issue I am dealing with?

Another variation on the treasure hunt is the scavenger hunt. This hunt is a little different in that you may start by creating a list of items you would like to find; for example, a feather, a leaf, a pinecone, a rock, a flower blossom, etc. Use your senses to track down these items as you hike.

A third variation is based on the use of the word *treasure* as a noun *or* a verb. You may choose to seek treasures, or you may notice or conjure memories of things (or people or places) that you treasure.

At the end of your treasure hunt or scavenger hunt, take a moment to contemplate your treasures. How did they get there? What were some of the processes that occurred in the creation and lifespan of the items that you found? How long was the journey that some of these items may have been on to land here? How old do you think they are? Are any of the items endangered or threatened? Why did they capture your attention? What else comes to mind about them? What else do you notice?

When you are ready to move on, find a safe spot away from the trail to return your treasures to the earth. You may feel like arranging them in some way. You may even feel the urge to thank them for their message and their teachings.

Plant Wisdom: Poison Ivy

Can you spot the "leaves of three"? Poison ivy, *Toxicodendron radicans*, can be found in just about every corner of the United States. This plant shares the noxious oil, called urushiol, with Pacific poison oak, Atlantic poison oak, and poison sumac, which have distributions in the western, southeastern, and eastern United States, respectively. Urushiol is found within the plant's sap and is the culprit behind the contact dermatitis, or allergic skin rash, that many nature lovers have experienced, prompting the saying "Leaves of three, let it be."

Urushiol binds to skin upon contact, leading to itching, inflammation, and blistering. Contrary to popular belief, the blisters caused by poison ivy, oak, and sumac do not contain urushiol. Rather, blisters contain a watery fluid, or transudate, that is a result of the body's immune response. Because of this, a person cannot transmit poison ivy via the fluid in the blisters from one body part to another or from person to person. One can, however, transmit the *oil* from one part of the body to another, as urushiol has the ability to stick around on skin and other surfaces for quite some time. The best defense against this transmission is washing with soap and water as soon as possible after contact occurs. Approximately 15 to 30 percent of people have no allergic response to poison ivy, but hundreds of thousands of individuals are affected by poison ivy annually in the United States.

Poison ivy can be identified by its classic "leaves of three" configuration. Often the two lateral leaves have a recognizable mitten-like shape. Each group of three leaflets grows on its own stem, which then connects to the main vine. Leaves are shiny and irregular but not serrated in shape. They turn red-orange in the fall. Poison ivy lacks thorns on the stem and can grow as a shrub, as well as a climbing or trailing vine.

From a conservation perspective, it is interesting to note that poison ivy often grows in disturbed areas (e.g., trails). I often think of it as the forest's barrier against human invaders, since animals and insects are not affected by its poisonous venom. More worrisome is the fact that poison ivy thrives on high carbon dioxide (CO_2) levels. With atmospheric changes from greenhouse emissions, poison ivy's prevalence and potency are expected to rise. Both have already doubled since the 1960s, according to the US Department of Agriculture, and could very likely double again in the next thirty to fifty years.

Deer Ears

One of the standard invitations taught to forest therapy guides is the invitation "Deer Ears." Simple as it is, it often elicits surprising revelations.

Animals have traits that make it very clear which sensory organs are most useful to them. Prey animals, like deer, have large ears and large eyes so they can remain on high alert for predators at all times. The auricle, or external ear, of mammals is designed as a funnel to bring sounds into the ear. Take a look at a human ear and notice how the cartilaginous whorls are suited for this purpose. Have you ever noticed how you instinctively cup your hand around your ear if you are trying to hear something better? It works! So, imagine if you had ears the size of deer ears.

Invitation: As you are walking down the trail, take both of your hands and raise them up to your ears. Cup your hands around the back of your ears to create larger auricles like those of a deer. Remember that no one is around to watch you (you probably will be more comfortable using this invitation in private or with others who will try it with you!), and continue down the trail for a period of time taking in the sounds of the forest using deer ears. What do you notice?

INVITATIONS AFTER HIKING
Cloud Stories

As a child, do you remember looking out of the car window at cloud shapes? Maybe (hopefully!) you even have memories of lying on the ground looking up at the clouds.

Invitation: After your hike, if conditions are appropriate, take a moment to lie down on a rock, log, or on the ground and simply look up at the clouds. Allow yourself to become lost in childlike imagination for a

while. What shapes do you notice? Do you see things like birds and animals? Notice how they mutate and transform before your very eyes. In your mind, invent a story of the transformation that is taking place before you. What do you notice about the way it makes you feel to watch and imagine stories in the clouds?

Sit Spot

Take some time, ideally twenty minutes, to incorporate "Sit Spot" into your forest bathing hike. Simply sit and take it all in, and notice what your senses bring forward. Notice the animals, birds, and insects minding their own business. Notice the plants and trees, and catch a twenty-minute glimpse into their day. It is easy to skip Sit Spot and rush off to

The Science of Nature: Grounding

Are you aware that there is an entire movement called "earthing" or "grounding"? This idea is based on the concept of simply spending time with exposed skin in contact with the ground, and that the negatively charged electrons from the surface of the earth are beneficial to our health. Examples of grounding include walking barefoot on the ground, sitting or lying on the ground or on sand or rocks, and even spending time in natural water.

We know that stressors in our environment (pesticides, herbicides, food additives, nicotine, alcohol, trans-fatty acids, and even emotional stress) contribute to the formation of free radicals in the body. Free radicals have been implicated in the aging process, the degeneration of tissue, the worsening of inflammation, and even the development of cancer. They occur when stable molecules are forced to lose an electron due to these stressors.

There is great interest and talk in health circles about the use of antioxidants. Antioxidants are substances that have *extra* electrons, so that when we ingest or use them, they can repair free radicals, thereby reversing the aging process and preventing inflammation, tissue degeneration, and tumor formation. Antioxidants include things like vitamins A, C, and E and phytonutrients in brightly colored fresh fruit and vegetables such as beta-carotene, lycopene, lutein, selenium, and epigallocatechin gallate, or EGCG (one of the chemicals in green tea), among many others. Preliminary studies suggest that spending time in direct contact with the ground offers some of the same health benefits as using or taking antioxidants in food or supplement form.

Other small studies have found that sleeping on the ground or on a commercial grounding pad speeds recovery from delayed onset muscle soreness (DOMS) from exercise (Brown et al. 2010), improves insomnia and decreases symptoms of depression and anxiety (Ghaly et al. 2004), and even increases the "zeta potential," or the electrical force between red blood cells, thereby decreasing inflammation, improving blood flow, decreasing the clumping of red blood cells, and reducing blood pressure (Chevalier et al. 2013). These studies are all presented in the book, *Barefoot Wisdom: Better Health through Grounding*, by Sharon Whitely and Ann Marie Chiasson, MD. Further studies are most certainly warranted, but with little risk involved in this intervention, why not give earthing a try?

our daily tasks. When we take the time to indulge in Sit Spot, though, there is always—without exception—a reward.

TEA CEREMONY: CHAMOMILE

Many people have heard of, or tried, chamomile tea. Many are surprised to learn that chamomile is an herb that can commonly be found growing in the wild. Because of this, it can be an excellent choice for a post-hike tea ceremony.

There are many forms of chamomile, members of the Asteraceae (or sunflower) family. Two of the forms that are commonly used medicinally are Roman chamomile (*Chamaemelum nobile*) and German chamomile (*Matricaria recutita*). Both tend to grow in dry areas with adequate sun, and both are found as nonnative transplants in various parts of the United States.

Because the Asteraceae family is so vast, chamomile may be confused with a number of other aster flowers, including ox-eye daisy and fleabane. Both German and Roman chamomile can be distinguished

from the other asters by the shape of the flower and the foliage. Chamomile's flowers have a raised yellow center, with white ray petals that, with age, hang down from the flower head. This is in contrast to the ox-eye daisy (*Leucanthemum vulgare*), which has a flatter (sometimes even sunken) yellow flower head with larger and longer white rays. Fleabane (*Erigeron annuus*), on the other hand, also has a yellow center and white rays, but again the center is less dome-shaped than chamomile's and the white rays spread outward or even upward. Additionally, fleabane has many more (around a hundred) very thin white rays, whereas chamomile and ox-eye daisy both have approximately twenty rays per flower head.

The leaves of both the Roman and German chamomile plants are finely dissected, fernlike, long, narrow lobes, as opposed to ox-eye daisy, which has larger, serrated whole leaves that are narrow at the base and wider at the tip. Fleabane also has whole, oblong, serrated leaves.

To summarize, if the aster plant you are contemplating has a domed yellow center with about twenty white rays that are either flat or hang downward, and its leaves are finely dissected and fernlike, you may have encountered chamomile.

The flower heads of chamomile (either fresh or dried) are typically used in tea; however, the leaf may also be used. It is considered very safe, with the only precaution being the potential for allergic cross-reaction in those who have allergies to ragweed.

Medicinally, chamomile has been used as a relaxant and mild sleep aid, a digestive aid, and an antispasmodic for treatment of colic in infants. Applied topically, it has even been found to be as effective as over-the-counter hydrocortisone cream for the treatment of eczema.

During the tea ceremony, consider paying tribute to the history of the Native lands upon which you hiked. Make a point to learn the

ancestral name of the area, and give thanks to the indigenous tribes who were the first to care for the land. Take a moment, also, to reflect upon your forest bathing hike. What will you bring back to your daily life?

In Closing

I often take photos of trails. There is something particularly alluring about gazing down a trail to the point where it vanishes into the horizon, around a corner, or down into a valley. To me, trails are metaphors of life. When I was in Tucson, studying integrative medicine, I would often hike alone on the Pima Canyon Trail. I took a photo, one time, that sits in my office where I see patients. Because I believe there is much more to healing than treating symptoms with pharmaceutical medications, I often talk with my patients about the journey of life and about the idea of life's purpose.

On many occasions, I have pointed to my photo of the trail at Pima Canyon and shared the realization I had one of the first times I hiked there: I was hot. There was no shade along the trail. The trail bed was rocky, and it was an uphill struggle. Every now and then I would trip on a root or a rock. There were cactuses and other prickly plants that seemed to reach out and scratch my arms and legs if I wasn't careful. I knew there could be snakes or other dangerous creatures that could hurt or even kill me. I wondered why I was even there, at times, when I could easily give up and get out of there.

But it felt good to be outdoors and to be alone with my thoughts, my sweat, and my heavy breathing. The trail drew me in and beckoned me forward. Suddenly, the trail rounded a curve. There was a lush canyon (hence the name!) that I had never imagined was there. All of a sudden there was shade and greenery. It was such a welcome reprieve and so overwhelmingly beautiful. I sat down and took it all in.

That metaphor for life—continuing to hike forward on the trail, in spite of the uphill, rocky struggle; realizing that taking calculated risks and facing challenges is necessary for attaining rewards and achieving goals along our journey—has stuck with me ever since.

PADDLING

My first memory of canoeing was at about the age of seven. It was a big deal, because a group of dads took their kids on an overnight canoe trip on the Upper Iowa River. There must have been about five or six dads and their kids, so it seemed like a pretty large group. There were little kids like my brother and me, and there were big, teenage kids. I remember wondering if the dads would know how to feed us, but it seems that we all survived. (I do recall eating Doritos and Twinkies!) We camped on the side of the river, and I remember waking up very cold.

I have a vivid memory of looking up at the tall limestone bluffs that line the Upper Iowa, and of the fascinating swallow nests that peppered these bluffs. I felt tiny, yet very liberated, down in that canoe. It was so peaceful and serene. I also recall a rush of fear and excitement when we encountered the small rapids on that river. I remember the second day ending way too soon and that I wanted to go paddling again.

When I think back to childhood experiences like this, I realize that—as with many people I have interviewed—I have loved adventure, been mesmerized by nature, and have practiced the art of *shinrin-yoku* for as long as I can remember.

History and Stewardship

Historically there have been countless iterations of the paddled vessel. According to the website of the International Canoe Federation (IFC; www.canoeicf.com), founded in 1924, "Wherever there is water, there is an indigenous watercraft. Mostly, this is in the form of a Canoe." Over time and throughout all corners of the globe, canoes have been built out of wood, animal skins, and later fabricated materials. It is believed that the kayak originated in Greenland (from the Eskimo term *ki ak*, meaning "man boat") as a one-man canoe with protection from the elements in the form of a covered cockpit. These boats have been used historically for transportation, fishing, and hunting, and even for war. Today, while canoes and kayaks continue to be used for many of these purposes, there is a growing interest in paddling as a form of recreation and sport. Rafting and stand-up paddleboards (SUPs) are included in the ever-growing list of popular paddling sports today.

A number of organizations support and govern the sport of paddling. ICF states that it represents the global canoeing movement and is composed of 5 continental and 164 national federations. It "supports the worldwide network of committed canoeing experts," including everything from the Olympic Games to local recreational paddling.

ICF is an official sponsor of Paddle for the Planet, an organization that hosts a worldwide relay "as a show of solidarity to protect the world's waterways and oceans and to raise funds for environmental conservation projects close to the paddlers' hearts," according to its website. Various paddling-related events, often involving waterway cleanup projects, are coordinated by paddlers using "canoes, kayaks, surf skis, dragon boats, outriggers and stand-up paddle boards in every corner of the globe." Initially held in 2012, twenty-eight nations

participated in Paddle for the Planet by the year 2017. For information on joining this cause, visit www.paddlefortheplanet.org.

Within the United States, at least two additional organizations govern the sport of paddling and are highly involved in conservation efforts. Founded in 1880, the mission of the American Canoe Association (ACA; www.americancanoe.org) involves "serving the broader paddling public by providing education related to all aspects of paddling; stewardship support to help protect paddling environments; and sanctioning of programs and events to promote paddlesport competition, exploration and recreation," according to its website. Similarly, the American Kayaking Association (AKA; www.americankayak.org) states its mission is to "accelerate America's growing passion for paddle sports and transform the paddling community into an educated and connected, conservation-based culture of stewardship for our most precious resource: Water." Both organizations also offer training and certification for individuals with physical disabilities in order to integrate them into the world of paddling activities and competitive sports.

There are also a number of organizations that support water conservation, as well as organizations that use water as therapy. Founded in 1915, and originally known as the Ecological Society of America, the Nature Conservancy (www.nature.org) works on a global level to preserve native land and water. "The Nature Conservancy's Saving Great Rivers program looks at entire river systems—from mountain headwaters to coastal deltas—to find solutions that support both humans and other species. That approach is helping China, Colombia and the United States, among other countries, sustain ecologically vibrant rivers that serve as a foundation for human prosperity and security, providing hydropower and other benefits to humans while supporting healthy ecosystems" (Bramen 2017).

For more than twenty years, Casting for Recovery has introduced breast cancer survivors to the outdoors through fly-fishing retreats at no cost to the participants. Currently under the direction of Whitney Milhoan, "CfR's retreats offer opportunities for women to find inspiration, discover renewed energy for life, and experience healing connections with other women and nature. The retreats are open to women with breast cancer of all ages, in all stages of treatment and recovery," Castingforrecovery.org. The physician in me has always been intrigued by the fact that the movement involved in fly fishing provides excellent physical therapy and lymphedema treatment following surgery and radiation for breast cancer.

Soul River (www.soulriverinc.org) provides veterans and at-risk youth fly-fishing and paddling experiences that act therapeutically for humans and waterways simultaneously. Founder Chad Brown, a decorated US Navy veteran who lives with post-traumatic stress disorder (PTSD), shared his story at the 2018 SHIFT festival in Jackson Hole, Wyoming. He credits his postwar survival to an unexpected opportunity to try fly fishing. He now enlists veterans to become mentors for at-risk youth in his outdoor program. As noted on the website, "Spending time embraced in currents of river water, trekking majestic forested trails, and witnessing a bald eagle or elk in its habitat is healing. Connecting with nature is a powerful outlet to reduce stress, find focus, sharpen self-awareness, embrace spirituality, and develop positive values beneficial to both the individual and community. Soul River unites youth and veterans on challenging yet rewarding adventures at zero cost where they become part of something bigger than themselves, developing into strong leaders in the outdoors and their communities." They return home "to themselves and their communities as inspired ambassadors of nature."

It is clear that organizations such as these have far-reaching and long-lasting effects. Please refer to the sidebar in this chapter for more information about the use of forest bathing for individuals with PTSD.

Mindfulness in Paddling

Paddlers tend to employ mindfulness, whether they realize it or not. The pattern of each stroke—placing the paddle, submerging it in the water, rotating the wrist, twisting the core, and drawing the paddle backward, then repeating on the other side, over and over as the boat is propelled forward—creates a rhythm that becomes almost trancelike in its repetition. In order to move the boat, concentration must be placed on each stroke, otherwise the boat stops moving.

In a small, local survey I conducted on the subject of kayaking and mindfulness, however, I was surprised to find that only 43 percent of respondents cited the repetitive motion of paddling to be a reason they achieve mindfulness in kayaking. As a matter of fact, 100 percent of respondents cited "being out in nature" as a factor that they believed contributed to mindfulness while kayaking, followed by the proximity

Special Populations: Forest Bathing for PTSD

Post-traumatic stress disorder, or PTSD, is a mental health condition that can develop after an individual experiences a traumatic event that is beyond the level of a typical stressor. The National Institute of Health's Medline Plus website (www.medlineplus.gov) reports that an estimated 7.7 million American adults are currently living with PTSD.

According to the National Institute of Mental Health (NIMH), events such as violent personal assaults, natural or human-caused disasters, accidents, combat, and other forms of violence may predispose a person to develop PTSD. Although it is common to be exposed to these forms of trauma, with around half of all American adults experiencing at least one traumatic event in their lives, most do not go on to develop PTSD. Individuals with PTSD may "have persistent, frightening thoughts and memories of the event(s), experience sleep problems, feel detached or numb, or may be easily startled. In severe forms, PTSD can significantly impair a person's ability to function at work, at home, and socially," according to the NIMH website (www.nimh.nih.gov).

Forest bathing has emerged as a potential therapeutic modality for individuals who live with PTSD. Below are two compelling stories shared by ANFT-certified forest therapy guides.

I'm guiding a client I'll call Doug in the woods, a former Secret Service agent and veteran of the Afghanistan war. You'd never guess it from his appearances as an expert on news panels or his fast-paced career in political administration, but his severe PTSD keeps him up at night. If sleep comes, it's riddled with nightmares. In the woods, I guide Doug through a few invitations. Birds call, cicadas drone lazily, the early fall breeze meanders through the trees with the same ease that Doug and I wander through our senses. After several months coming out forest bathing with me, Doug has become adept at learning to redirect himself when he feels triggered. A restful awareness visibly relaxes his body in stark contrast to the rigid hypervigilance he arrived with today. Doug rummages

through the deep pockets of his cargo pants. He lays out an aston-
ishing display on the forest floor: two guns, a pocketknife, a small
can of pepper spray, a marijuana vaporizer, a one-hitter pipe, a
baggie filled with marijuana, two packs of cigarettes and a lighter, a
flask, and a small bowie knife in a sheath.

"I want to see what it's like without carrying that weight," he
explains. "Usually I need to carry this to feel prepared or protected,
but I don't think I need it right now." I've worked with lots of clients,
but this is the first time I've seen someone literally disarm himself.
Doug hops up with the enthusiasm and curiosity of a kid. Leaving
his cache of weapons and numbing agents, he lopes over to a fallen
tree, climbs up, and balances one foot in front of the other. He
unearths a fist-size rock, which he grasps with two hands overhead,
seizing it with all his might until his whole body trembles. He hurls
it into the creek, where it lands with a satisfying KER-SPLOOSH. He
grins back at me. There's plenty of space for him out here.

(Clare Kelley is a trauma-informed forest therapy guide in Washington, DC.)

***

I had this realization on day seven in my weeklong intensive to
become a forest therapy guide with ANFT:

As a person who lives with PTSD, I noticed that it had been the
longest in over twenty years that those intrusive trauma thoughts
didn't come . . . AT ALL. I had experienced, firsthand, the power
that exists in immersing yourself into the more-than-human world.
The most impressive part was that the effect stayed with me for
more than twenty days after my training. I was able to take that
home with me and practice it. My husband is a veteran also living
with PTSD, and seeing the joy he receives from forest therapy has
been amazing. Being able to connect and feel is so important in the
healing journey and in overall quality of life and well-being. Having
the opportunity to allow for the sharing and openness that occurs in
forest bathing has been life changing. I am forever grateful.

(Leigh-Anne Lisi is a certified forest therapy guide in Jacques,
Ontario, Canada.)

Anna Levesque is an athlete whose credentials speak for themselves on the topic of mindfulness and outdoor adventure. The author of *Yoga for Paddling*, Anna is an RYT 500 yoga instructor, an ACA level 5 whitewater kayak instructor, an ACA level 4 whitewater kayak instructor trainer, an ACA level 2 SUP instructor trainer, and an ACA SUP yoga instructor, as well as a certified Ayurveda wellness counselor.

When asked about her application of mindfulness practices in her various paddling ventures, Anna had much to contribute: "Whitewater kayaking, like the breath, gives access to the present moment. A successful run through a rapid requires that the paddler see the path as it is, with nothing left out and nothing added. From that place of paying attention in the moment without judgment, right action can be taken. The moment a paddler enters a rapid everything else falls away and there is only the present moment, the path in front of you and the action needed. Some call this the 'flow state' or being in the flow or even freedom. I think one of the reasons whitewater kayaking is so compelling to some people is this present moment access."

She went on to say, "It's the same when catching a wave in paddle surfing. Watching the swell, positioning yourself at the peak of the wave, and then focusing on the action needed in the moment to catch the wave. Riding a wave down the line and maneuvering requires constant paying attention to what is happening now, and now, and now. There is no time to think about anything else, and when you do, when the mind wanders or gets fearful, that's when you wipe out!

"Flatwater stand-up paddleboarding can also be a beautiful practice in mindfulness," she continued. "The quiet, the sound of the paddle entering and exiting the water, the feeling of the body strong and activated, awareness of the mind calm and peaceful."

Regarding the combination of yoga and paddling, she added, "Practicing yoga on stand-up paddleboards is one of the most joyful mindfulness exercises that I've experienced. It's an exercise in noticing what is happening now. We get to take in the qualities of the Five Elements and remember that we are nature. Moving between paying attention to our balance on the board and floating relaxation is very healing for people."

I asked Anna if specific sensory elements in nature seemed to help her achieve mindfulness. She replied, "It's my experience that some outdoor enthusiasts hit the water, the trail, the wall, and the mountain with a specific goal in mind. Our culture is so achievement oriented that even those who love to get out in nature get attached to outcome instead of paying attention to what is happening now. I think practices like yoga, meditation, and forest bathing have a lot to contribute to outdoor enthusiasts."

She continued to share: "In between rapids I breathe deeply and take the time to notice patterns in the water, wildlife by the river, leaves falling, wind blowing through, the sounds of the water. I also love to take in all the colors and beauty. This helps me to reset, feel grateful, and prepare for the next rapid.

"When I'm in the ocean I give thanks to the water spirits and all life living in the ocean. I ask that all those surfing and/or paddling that day be kept safe. When I'm waiting for a set to roll in I focus on the rise and fall of the ocean swell and connect it to the flow in my own body. Paddle surfing at sunrise and sunset makes it easy to practice mindfulness and take in the colors, the beauty, and say 'thank you for my life.'

"Practicing mindfulness while I'm paddling and also having paddling be a mindfulness practice helps me to fully experience the joy of being grateful for my life and my journey on this Earth walk. Gratitude for life, there is no greater gift."

to water (67 percent) and being alone in the kayak (57 percent) (participants were asked to mark all factors that they believed contributed to mindfulness).

In my survey, some of the other factors that contributed to mindfulness included the "calming sound as the paddle cuts and moves the water," "the unique sensation of movement on water vs. land—smooth, gliding, no-impact," and being "physically removed from distractions on land." Additionally, "Gliding through the water is so effortless and quiet. The silent movement gives me peace."

Eighty-six percent of respondents to my small survey revealed that they usually feel "less stress, anxiety, and/or depression" after kayaking, as opposed to 5 percent who said they felt more stress, anxiety, and/or depression and 10 percent who have never noticed a change in their mental status after kayaking. One participant wrote, "It is like a reset sometimes, especially when I spend a longer time on the water. I go from mind over-activity to a highly salient feeling of groundedness. Afterward, the effect can last for days, keeping me grounded in purposeful pursuits." Based on my small survey, paddling seems like a pretty good mental health prescription, without the risk of side effects or drug interactions!

FOREST BATHING/SHINRIN-YOKU AND PADDLING

INVITATIONS BEFORE PADDLING
Pleasures of Presence

Completing the "Pleasures of Presence" invitation before setting out to paddle can set the tone for your entire day. Situate yourself so that you can sit down right next to the water, close enough that you are able to reach out and touch it. This may be on a dock, a boat ramp, or the

shore. If this is not possible, find a quiet place where you can sit close enough to see the water and modify the invitation as needed.

Invitation: Start by closing your eyes and taking a few slow, deep breaths. Feel yourself rooted to the earth in this place, near the water. Imagine for a moment that you are sitting here a few hundred years ago. What might it have been like back then? Did humans inhabit this region at that time? Do you know the names of any of the indigenous tribes of people who lived in this area? What was the ancestral name of this place where you are sitting? If you don't know the ancestral name of this place or the name of the indigenous people who lived here, make a mental note to look up this information at a later time. Can you imagine Native ancestors settling near this body of water? How do you suppose they used the water in their everyday life? How do you suppose the water was valued or revered by these people? Might it have been viewed as sacred?

Return your focus to your breathing and, again, take some slow, deep breaths. Prolong your exhalations and notice your body and mind begin to let go of any tension. Notice that by breathing in the air that is near this body of water, you are breathing in molecules of evaporated water. You are, in essence, breathing the water into your body.

Cup your hands and dip them into the water, holding the water in your hands. Take as much time as you need between each observation. Begin by noticing the temperature of the water compared to your hands. How does it compare? Then examine the weight of the water. Does it surprise you to consider the weight of water? Allow the water to run through your fingers. What does this feel like? Is there any particulate matter in the water or does it feel clean? Bring the water up to your chin or even your lips, if you wish. Notice the sensation of the water touching your face. What do you notice? As you pass the water between your hands and fingers, imagine where it has been. Where did it come from? How long has it been flowing through Earth's waterways? Can you imagine it coming down from the clouds as rain? Where will it go next? Imagine all of the plants, animals, fish, insects, rocks, and sand that this water has touched. Contemplate, for a moment, the life force energy that is water.

Next, bring your ear down to your cupped hands and listen to the water. Does water in your cupped hands make a sound? Allow the water to filter through your fingers and splash back into the river, lake, or onto the ground. What does this sound like? You may wish to gather more water and allow it to splash back down, over and over, a few times. Feel free to do this, and remind yourself to focus on the sounds the water makes. If you are distracted by other senses, gently return your attention to the sounds of the water. Next, with eyes closed and hands empty, notice the sounds of the water around you. Is it a loud, rushing sound? Is it still? Is it somewhere in between? Is the sound continuous or sporadic? What are the forces that cause the sounds you are hearing? Do you hear any rhythms in the sounds of the water? How about the pitch of the sounds the water makes—are they high- or low-pitched? Have you ever thought about that before? Do the sounds remind you of anything? What is the first thought that comes to mind when you contemplate a memory of these sounds? What else do you notice about the sounds of water?

Now, begin to notice your sense of smell. Take a large inhale and breathe in the scent of the water around you. What do you notice? Take a few more breaths, simply noticing the smells of the body of water in front of you. Again, take some water into your hands and bring it up to your face so that you can get a closer experience of the scent of the water. What do you notice now? After you release the water again, notice the smell of the water on your hands. Do any thoughts or memories arise?

A taste of the water may or may not be advised. In pristine circumstances, you may actually wish to taste the water. Use common sense on this one!

Finally, prepare to open your eyes and view this body of water as if you have never seen it, or anything like it, before. Give yourself a count of three, and then open your eyes. What do you notice about water, and specifically this body of water, when you gaze upon it as if for the very first time? Spend as much time as you wish, simply taking it all in. When you feel complete, consider taking a moment to journal or jot some notes about your experience. If you are doing this with other people, take a moment to share some observations with one another about the Pleasures of Presence with water.

What's in Motion?

As forest bathing guides, we often strive to incorporate moving water into the invitation "What's in Motion?," making it the ideal invitation to use prior to setting out in a kayak, raft, SUP, or canoe.

Invitation: While you sit or stand next to the water, plan to spend ten minutes or so simply noticing what is in motion. You may find yourself spending the entire time watching the movement of the water, or you may be drawn to notice other things in motion within your sight, such as birds and waterfowl, insects, animals, or the movements of the plants on the edge of the water. Afterward, share your experience with another person, or take a moment to journal or jot some notes about the experience of viewing motion.

Float a Wish

No need to wait until your next birthday cake! Before setting out on your paddling adventure (and provided your body of water has current, wind, or surf), take a moment to bring to mind your deepest heart's desire. As T. S. Eliot said, "Sometimes things become possible if we want them bad enough."

Invitation: Pick up a lightweight object, such as a leaf or a feather. Close your eyes, make a wish, and make a pact with yourself that you will take just one step toward bringing your dream to fruition. Share your wish and your pact with your leaf or feather, and then release it into the water. As you watch your wish floating away, imagine the Universe conspiring to help you. Try to keep your eye on the object until it leaves your line of sight. Close your eyes and feel the sensation in your body that you will experience when your dream comes true. When you are ready to open your eyes, do so. If you are able, take a moment to jot down your wish and your pact.

INVITATIONS DURING PADDLING
Pleasures of Presence

Just as completing the invitation "Pleasures of Presence" can be an effective way to "drop in" to the space prior to embarking on a paddling adventure, this invitation is perfectly suited to be used *while* paddling.

Many paddlers comment that they find a rhythm in their paddle strokes. Sometimes it can take a while before one can settle into this rhythm, so why not bring your attention to the rhythm of the stroke right off the bat?

Invitation: While you are paddling, begin by noticing the way the water looks as the paddle cuts into it, first on the right, then the left, then the right, then the left, and so on, if you are kayaking. In a canoe, raft, or SUP, see if you can create rhythm while paddling on each side of your vessel. Attempt to keep your attention on the visual aspect of the paddle slicing into the water. Notice the effect the paddle has on the surface of the water, and then notice the water's movement as it drips off the paddle: right, left, right.

Next, notice the way the paddle *feels* as it moves through the water, first entering the water, then drawing backward, and then exiting the water. Notice the tactile sensation of each component of the stroke. Attempt to balance this tactile sensation: right, left, right. Allow your body to fall into a steady rhythm. Notice the way the muscles and joints of your upper body feel as you paddle through the water. As your rhythm becomes established, notice the sounds the paddle makes with each stroke: right, left, right. How does each separate portion of the paddle stroke *sound*?

Expand your awareness, now, to the space around you. Continue the mindful paddling rhythm, but soften your gaze to take in your entire surroundings. Notice the colors you are able to absorb, all

at once. Is there an overabundance of shades of a particular color, say green or brown? Attempt to take in as many shades of one color as possible, all at once. What is it like to do this? Do you notice any visual patterns? Are there areas of darkness versus areas that are brighter? What happens if you squint your eyes and examine the world in this way?

Now, begin to notice the sounds around you. Continue to notice the background sounds of the paddle moving through the water, and begin to take in the other sounds that are in your midst. Notice, first, the sound of your breathing, and focus on this for a while. Then, notice the ambient sounds of the water. Is there a current? Is the water still? Even if there is little movement, is there still a sound that the water makes? Take some time to notice these sounds. Notice, next, the sounds of the wind moving through trees, grasses, and shrubs on land. Focus on these sounds for a while, before starting to listen for the sounds of birds, insects, and animals nearby. Notice sounds of wildlife that are much farther away. Try to separate these natural sounds from each other and then from other ambient, perhaps man-made, sounds.

Finally, bring your attention to your olfactory sense. What do you smell? Is there a scent from your clothing or your life jacket? What other scents do *you* bring to your environment? Can you notice the smell of your paddle and your boat? Next, what does the water smell like? What about the air? Do the fragrances change as you move forward through the water? Are you able to smell any trees, flowers, or grasses?

You may choose to focus on a particular sense for a period of time as you paddle: sight, smell, hearing. I often choose about twenty minutes for each sense before moving on to another one. Doing this for a set period of time can bring you deeper into a state of mindfulness and enhance your paddling experience.

What's in Motion?

As the invitation "What's in Motion?" works well before a paddling adventure, it also works well during the activity.

Invitation: As you paddle, simply notice what is in motion in nature. One can spend a great deal of time simply observing the movement of the water. Current, rapids, eddies, waves, and wakes from other boats can be mesmerizing to watch. Notice the movement of animals and birds, trees, and other plants as you paddle. Notice your own movement in the scheme of it all. What thoughts or feelings arise?

The Water's Edge

Following a linear focal point can be soothing and settling to the mind. This invitation not only quiets the mind, but can even settle the stomach for those who happen to suffer from seasickness on a boat.

Invitation: Look at the line where the water meets the shore. How far can you follow that line from your left, all the way to the horizon? How far can you follow the shoreline on your right, all the way to the horizon? Make it a point to move your eyes as slowly as possible from the shoreline adjacent to you all the way to the horizon, or as far as you can see. This invitation is best performed as you sit stationary in your boat, but can be done while paddling as long as you are able to check in front of you, periodically, as you go. What do you notice as you survey the water's edge in this way?

Go Deep

Especially suited for stand-up paddleboarding, but also completely amenable to other forms of paddling, this invitation offers depth in more ways than one.

Invitation: Start by looking at the surface of the water, right next to your boat. Are there large items such as leaves or other plant debris floating on the surface? Watch these items as they move and flow with the surface of the water, and notice how the movement of your boat affects this.

Now, attempt to inspect the contents of the water within the first five to ten inches below the surface, and notice what you are seeing. Are there plants, such as reeds, kelp, or seaweed, just beneath the surface? Look at any large items beneath the surface and examine their color, texture, movement, and interaction with other plant or animal life. Speaking of which, are there any fish, reptiles, amphibians, or other creatures just below the surface? What are they doing? Do they seem to react to your presence, or do they go about their business unaffected by you?

Next, notice any tiny material in this top layer of water. Is there particulate matter that you are able to visualize? Does the angle of the

Herbal Insight: Cattail

Did you know that cattails (*Typha lati-folia*)—those spiky, fuzzy, brown plants that line marshes, ditches, and bodies of water—are not only edible but offer a number of medicinal properties? This does come with a caveat, though, so keep reading.

Historically, depending on the season, different parts of the cattail have been eaten in a variety of ways. In spring, the stalks can be eaten raw or cooked like asparagus. In late spring, the green flower spikes can be boiled, buttered, and eaten like sweet corn. In early summer, the pollen can be gathered and used as a protein-rich flour, mixed half and half with wheat flour.

Medicinally, the roots and shoots are useful. A gel found at the base of the roots has been found to have both antiseptic and soothing properties, and therefore has been used as a topical agent for burns and stings. Over time, cattail pollen has been used internally to control nosebleeds, uterine bleeding, and blood in the urine. When its herbal actions have been studied, cattail has been found to have diuretic, expectorant, antibacterial, antihelminth, antimicrobial, and emetic properties. In other words, it can make you produce urine; make you cough; can fight bacteria, worms, and other types of infections; and can induce vomiting (such as in cases of accidental poisoning).

So, here's the caveat: Cattail does a terrific job as a natural water filter. It absorbs contaminants and toxins, including arsenic. This is great for the water and the ecosystem, but means that eating cattail might mean ingesting poisonous toxins. For this reason, it is extremely important to know the body of water from which you are harvesting—it should probably be left to the experts.

Even if we don't make it a practice to forage cattail from our local ponds, lakes, and rivers, it is nice to know that this diligent plant is working to detoxify our water!

sun or presence of light versus shade change your ability to see these tiny things? Are they alive? Do they appear to represent plant or animal life? How tiny are these beings, and how many of them could be living within your field of vision? Are you able to see anything that is even smaller than these?

Finally, take your gaze as far down into the water as you are able to see. Can you see the bottom of this body of water? Can you make out sand, rocks, dirt, shells, coral, or other natural objects that line the riverbed, lake bottom, or ocean floor? Do those items move or are they stationary? If they are moving, what are the forces that cause that motion? Do you see fish or other beings at the depths of the water? Can you see the base of any plants that are rooted down below? How many different signs of life can you spot deep, deep down? Spend as much time as you like contemplating the visual experience of different depths of the water. What is it like to go deep?

Circles of Life

So many circles! Anyone who has spent time on the water knows that a fish jumping out of the water creates a perfect circle of water when it splashes back down. Skipping rocks leaves a parade of little circular splashes before the rock finally sinks. Have you ever noticed just how many circles appear on the surface of water?

Invitation: Particularly mesmerizing on a drizzly day, any conditions will do for this invitation. Take a few moments to scan the very surface of the water. This can be done while paddling or while stopped for a break. Look for the telltale signs that something has breached the surface of the water, either from above or below. Notice from which direction this breach may have occurred. Is there something falling from above: precipitation, water droplets from your paddle, leaves or other plant material falling from trees? Is something rising from below: air bubbles from submerged animal or plant life; fish, animals, or insects grazing the surface? Notice how many of these circles are present simultaneously as you skim the surface as far as the eye can see. Watch the ripples expand until they disappear. What else do you notice about these circles of life in the water?

Floating Reflections

In still water, seeing the world's reflection is like staring at a Monet painting. It's also where the word *reflection* can have more than one meaning.

Invitation: As you are paddling next to a tree-lined shore, a bluff, a coastal cliff, a cavern, or any other overhang, invite yourself to explore a different viewpoint. Look into the water at the reflection of the underside of the trees, bluff, cavern, or cliff. Do you also see clouds in the sky that are reflected in the water? How does this mirror image, and looking downward at it, differ from the perspective you are used to seeing? Can you capture both the actual object and its reflection at the same time? Do you notice details in the reflection that you may have otherwise missed? What effect does the water have on the image? What else do you notice? What does it mean to "reflect"?

Stretch Your Body, Stretch Your Mind

After a few hours of paddling, the upper body can start to feel it. In a kayak, I love to raise my paddle over my head and stretch my back over the hull of the boat. This could be modified on a canoe, SUP, or raft with some balance and creativity.

Invitation: While floating in an area that is safe from other watercraft or other hazards, take a moment to raise your paddle over your head with straightened arms. Feel the stretch in the back of your neck, shoulders, upper back, and arms. If your flexibility allows, arch all the way backward until you can rest your back on the hull of the kayak (or modify according to your boat). If you are prone to motion sickness, fix your gaze on a nonmoving object like a tree or bluff. Take a moment to view the expansive horizon, the clouds, and the infinite sky. How does this make you feel?

INVITATIONS AFTER PADDLING

Sit Spot

The invitation "Sit Spot" is appropriate after any activity, and a paddling adventure is no exception, as open water offers some of the best contemplative experiences. Once you have taken care of getting your boat out of the water and securing your equipment, take twenty minutes to enjoy Sit Spot.

Find a comfortable spot on the ground, a bench, a rock, or a log and take it all in. What do you notice about your sit spot? What observations do you have? Are there any findings that relate to your life in some way? Are there any metaphors in paddling that apply to a question or problem you have been working with? Did reflections and depths provoke memories or glimpses of insight? What thoughts, emotions, or ideas arise from Sit Spot? Remember to take time to journal or jot a few notes following Sit Spot.

TEA CEREMONY: STINGING NETTLE

Many people have discovered stinging nettle's plant medicine by accident. This plant commonly lines trails and waterways and offers a memorable stinging burn, for about thirty minutes, for humans who trespass through its habitat. Forest bathers are often surprised to learn that this burn is disarmed when stinging nettle is transformed into a tea.

Stinging nettle, or *Urtica dioica* (from the Latin *urere*, meaning "to burn"; *urticaria* means "hives"), is native to Eurasia and North America. It can be recognized, if not by its sting, by its tall (two to six feet high) stalks of spiky leaves and flowers. It is often found in large patches, as it spreads by underground creeping rhizomes. Stinging nettle has tiny, needlelike hairs covering all parts of the plant with the exception of its roots. Upon the slightest contact, a chemical is released from these hairs that produces the stinging rash.

Since the time of Hippocrates in the fourth century BC, healers have used the burning effects of stinging nettle to fight fire with fire, so to speak, by applying it to painful areas of the body and confusing the transmission of pain signals to the brain. Today, stinging nettle is used to treat seasonal allergies, arthritis, and even benign prostatic hyperplasia (BPH). Research has confirmed and continues to explore the

efficacy of and mechanisms behind these healing properties. In fact, one study found that men with enlarged prostate who took 300 milligrams of stinging nettle root extract twice daily had improvement in urinary flow after eight weeks of use (Ghorbani et al. 2013).

To use stinging nettle for a tea ceremony, *definitely* wear gloves and long sleeves for harvesting. Fill a vessel with nettle leaves, pour nearly boiling water over them, steep for five to ten minutes, and enjoy. Trust in the fact that the hot water disarms the stinging properties, and notice your reaction to drinking stinging nettle tea.

A single cup of stinging nettle tea is not likely to cause any health issues for people; however, interactions are possible with some blood pressure, diabetes, anxiety, and insomnia medications.

During your tea ceremony, reflect on the area's watershed. Do you know how this body of water came to be here? If it is a lake, where does the water enter it? Does it exit? What forces created the depression in

The Science of Nature: It's Not Just Child's Play!

Watch some kids playing next to a shallow creek and, before long, chances are they will be floating leaves, nutshells, and tree bark down the stream as miniature boats.

A study from 2006 found that children who were enrolled in an outdoor kindergarten, in regular contact with nature, invented new games and forms of play 58 percent of the time, whereas those who took part in standard, indoor kindergarten invented new games only 16 percent of the time (Vigsø and Nielsen 2006).

Although most of us inherently know that children need outdoor time for creativity and mental stimulation, this and other studies are helping to quantify just how important it really is.

the earth that created this lake? If a river or creek flows into the lake, what feeds *that* river or creek? How far can you trace it back in your mind? If you are paddling on a river, do you know where the water goes next? Can you trace it in your mind all the way to an ocean? Do you know anything about the water table beneath the land on which you are sitting? Did you know that water found deep inside the water table has often been there for centuries? And if you paddled on the ocean, do you know any of the tributaries nearby that feed directly into the ocean? In your mind, can you follow them back to other riverways in which you have paddled before?

In what ways are natural waterways important to you, to our future, to the more-than-human world? Are there things that we, as humans, are doing to harm them? How can we do better?

In Closing

The paddling adventures I have had since that first canoe trip, many years ago, are now too numerous to count. As a child I went on additional family canoe trips, and I've taken my own kids on several. It makes me laugh to think back on some of my kids' character-building paddling adventures, like the time when they were two and four years old and my overzealous husband, Dave, shoved us off, tipping me right into the lake. Both kids were safe down inside the canoe but cried in fear, for the entire outing, that their mom might fall in the lake again! Then there was the whitewater rafting trip in Pennsylvania that embarked during a highly dismal downpour, the exhausting several-mile kayak outing at Minnesota's Gunflint Lake that ended in a thunderstorm, and the infamous Cedar River "kayak trip from hell" that was nine miles of paddling into a twenty-five-mile-per-hour headwind. My kids have always been troupers, but it's possible their mother overcommitted from time to time.

In spite of it all, I will never forget witnessing both my kids' sense of freedom as they took off on kayaks all by themselves on the shallow pond behind our house. At ages seven and nine, it was a pretty magnificent moment of independence. I couldn't help but notice them engaging with the water, plants, and wildlife in an innate forest bathing way.

Here's hoping there will be some happy childhood paddling memories for them too, and here's to all parents who instill early childhood nature connections in their children.

Crested Butte, Colorado

MOUNTAIN BIKING

There is no form of outdoor adventure that I love more than mountain biking. My first experience was with my dad, sometime in the nineties. My parents had given me a fully rigid dark purple Bianchi Osprey mountain bike for my college graduation, but I didn't really grasp the concept of "mountain biking." Initially, I just loved that I could zip up steep, paved hills on it. Then one day, on a bike ride with my dad, he made a sudden left turn onto a dirt trail at George Wyth State Park. "What?!" I thought. "I didn't know these trails existed! Can you *do* this?!" I was pretty cautious but beguiled by this revelation. I remember the thrill of riding on dirt and the apprehension of squeezing between narrow trees. And then that was that. It would be at least fifteen more years before I rode singletrack again.

During the summer of 2012, while training to run a half marathon, I decided to do my first eco-triathlon: mountain biking, trail running, and kayaking. I had been following these events for a few years and, since I had been running and kayaking a lot, I figured "How hard can mountain biking be?" Well, it turned out that I was completely ill-prepared for the mountain bike leg, *but* . . . it was the most fun I had had in years. I crashed a few times on that old nineties bike, so I was covered with mud and blood by the time I finished . . . and I was completely hooked.

Since that first eco-tri, I've spent hours and hours on (upgraded) mountain bikes and joined a great community of local riders. In her mysterious ways, the Universe introduced me to my husband, Joe, during a local group ride in 2015. Our 2016 outdoor wedding naturally included our fat bikes, which we rode down the proverbial aisle in our wedding attire. Mountain biking is a huge part of the fabric of our lives, and we have ridden and/or raced in nineteen states and Mexico at the time of this writing.

For me, mountain biking has become my favorite way to see the beautiful, wild places of the world. Exploring different terrain and getting well off the grid is magical. I find that the combination of mountain biking and forest bathing is very effective at improving my mountain biking agility and finding my "flow," and is generally a fabulous way to connect two of the things I love: riding singletrack and immersing myself in nature.

In one example of combining the two, I discovered that walking barefoot on a mountain bike trail is emotionally moving. A similar effect was expressed by others when I led a group of mountain bikers in forest bathing. On one such occasion, I stepped barefoot onto singletrack trail and noticed that I was walking upon deer tracks. I had this sudden visceral, awe-filled realization that my skin was touching the soil just the same as the animals and other beings with whom we share this trail. Sharing the story does no justice to the poignancy of the moment. It brought tears to my eyes and profoundly united my soul to that trail.

History and Trail Stewardship

Mountain biking, as it exists today, was born in the late 1960s to early 1970s. A British cyclist named Geoff Apps began building a lightweight

Fruita, Colorado

bicycle suited to off-road conditions in England in 1968. In the United States, riders in Marin County, California, claim rights to the sport's origination, but it was not until the late 1970s that mountain bikes were made commercially available.

Today, mountain bikers can be found riding dirt trails known as singletrack, fire roads, downhill ski trails, and backcountry roads. The sport lends itself well to outdoor enthusiasts aiming to escape urban life, pavement, and the hazards of bicycling in traffic.

One of the first mountain biking organizations was the National Off Road Bicycle Association, or NORBA, founded in 1983. This organization initially governed mountain bike racing in the United States and later was absorbed by USA Cycling (USAC).

In 1988 the International Mountain Bicycling Association (IMBA) was founded. Early on, this group worked to develop rules of the trail that are used nationwide today to ensure safe access for hikers, horseback riders, and mountain bikers on multiuse trails. Since its inception, IMBA has strived to collaborate with the Bureau of Land Management, the US Forest Service, and other organizations to protect natural areas and promote responsible biking on public lands. Low-impact riding, grassroots advocacy, sustainable trail design, innovative land management practices, and cooperation among trail user groups are all values that are promoted by IMBA. Today, IMBA consists of more than 200 chapters with over 40,000 individual members.

In the United States alone, there are over 65,000 miles in more than 21,000 trails that are designated for mountain biking, with this number increasing every year. Thanks to websites and apps such as MTB Project (www.mtbproject.com), mountain bikers can easily research and locate these trails.

A common thread among mountain biking and other trail-using organizations is that of the importance of trail stewardship. It is tragic to realize that some of the original mountain biking trails in Marin County, for example, have been destroyed by early mountain bikers to the point that mountain biking is no longer allowed on them. It is incumbent that those who utilize public trails become the greatest guardians of these treasures. Thankfully, in many parts of the country, mountain bikers are some of the staunchest advocates of conservation and trail protection. A practice of forest bathing is an excellent way to connect to the trails in a deeper, more meaningful way. Once cyclists discover this practice, they will find that incorporating its elements can even help pass the time while shoveling, raking, mowing, and weed-whacking!

The National Forest System Trails Stewardship Act, signed into law by President Obama in 2016, was designed to use existing resources within the Forest Service to increase the role of volunteers and partners in maintaining the usability and sustainability of the national forest trail system. Prior to the introduction of this act, the Forest Service was able to maintain only a quarter of the nearly 160,000 miles of national forest trails available for mountain biking, hiking, horseback riding, and other outdoor activities. This act allowed the use of volunteers and partners who maintain trails to be maximized and alleviated concerns for liability of these volunteers, all without the need for additional federal funding. IMBA supported the National Forest System Trails Stewardship Act, along with Backcountry Horsemen of America, the Wilderness Society, American Horse Council, American Hiking Society, American Motorcyclist Association, Trout Unlimited, and Partnership for the National Trails System, among others.

For the individual mountain bicyclist, trail stewardship (as defined by IMBA) involves:

- Respecting the landscape by remaining on trails and practicing "Leave No Trace" principles. This includes choosing not to ride on wet and muddy trails, causing rutting and widening of trails.

- Sharing the trail with other users and yielding to horses and foot traffic on multiuse trails.

- Riding open, legal trails as opposed to poaching trails, building illegal singletrack, and adding unauthorized trail features.

- Riding in control and avoiding trail conflict caused by being rude and inattentive or by riding too fast.

- Planning ahead to be prepared and self-sufficient. This involves carrying tools and supplies for flat tires and minor repairs, as well as carrying maps and GPS navigation apps.

- Minding animals and wildlife.

When mountain bikers and other trail users invest their personal time into trail maintenance, a relationship is fostered. One cannot help but see trails and natural spaces in a different light after a day of hard work and tender loving care. A similar experience is had when one spends a day forest bathing on or near a mountain biking trail—never will the term "shredding trail" be used so carelessly again.

Mindfulness in Mountain Biking

The term "mindfulness" is defined by Jon Kabat-Zinn, PhD, founder of the concept of Mindfulness-Based Stress Reduction, as "paying attention in a particular way: on purpose, in the present moment, and nonjudgmentally," and is quite the buzzword these days. But it does not take much stretching of the imagination to realize that bringing one's awareness to and focusing on the activity at hand is a technique that would improve safety in a sport such as mountain biking.

Additionally, achieving a state of "flow" is, after all, really the goal of such an activity. Psychologist Mihaly Csikszentmihalyi describes "flow" as "the mental state of operation in which a person performing an activity is fully immersed in a feeling of energized focus, full involvement, and enjoyment in the process of the activity. In essence, flow is characterized by complete absorption in what one does, and a resulting loss in one's sense of space and time . . . the state in which people are so involved in an activity that nothing else seems to matter; the experience itself is so enjoyable that people will do it even at great cost, for the sheer sake of doing it." He goes on to explain, "Concentration is so intense that there is no attention left over to think about anything irrelevant, or to worry about problems. Self-consciousness disappears, and the sense of time becomes distorted. An activity that produces such experiences is so gratifying that people are willing to do it for its own sake, with little concern for what they will get out of it, even when it is difficult, or dangerous." (From Csikszentmihalyi 1990.) Losing oneself for hours in a state of flow on a mountain bike is undoubtedly what keeps many of us practicing skills and seeking new trails.

Mountain biking, while sometimes involving considerable speed, can be a time to slow down and take in one's surroundings. While on a bike, it is much easier to absorb sights, smells, and sounds than it is while driving a motorized vehicle. With most Americans spending much more time in buildings and in cars, it is worth taking advantage of such a sensory opportunity.

It is difficult not to recognize the physical advantages of mindfulness. Have you ever lost yourself completely in a flow state while biking, only to realize you effortlessly achieved a new personal record? Conversely, have you spent time on a treadmill witnessing every minute slog by, ultimately cutting your workout short out of pure misery? Enough said.

As for brain fitness, mindfulness practices have been largely accepted as beneficial for brain health and improving memory and cognition. Although of questionable veracity, folklore holds that Albert Einstein came up with his theory of relativity while riding a bike. Maybe he did, maybe he didn't, but have you ever had a flash of insight while mountain biking? I know I have.

Finally, a practice of mindfulness furthers a sense of trail stewardship and connection with nature. As Buddhist monk Thich Nhat Hanh states, "Mindfulness shows us what is happening in our bodies, our emotions, our minds, and in the world. Through mindfulness, we avoid harming ourselves and others."

My friend, yoga teacher, and avid mountain biker Mary McInnis, MA, RYT 500, sums up her connection to nature as this: "When I am on my mountain bike in the woods, it's not about moments of exhilaration. It's about the opposite—the constancy inherent in the experience. The way time doesn't have a hold on me anymore, nature does, and it knows no time. The place surrounds me, moves into me, and steadies me."

She goes on to say, "I'm not 'appreciating' nature in an active sense, I'm simply letting nature do its work on me—the smells, the sounds, the sensations. I am happy and smiling and sometimes even letting out a whoop, but none of it feels temporary. It feels like the thing that has always been, in the place that has always been, around me and within me."

Sage Raindancer is a mountain biker as well as an urban cyclist. "I'm a commuter, volunteer bike marshal, former professional urban cyclist aka 'bike courier,' and a bike instructor," he says. "I do believe that training, recreating, and working outdoors does factor in when being mindful, for me."

"I think of it like this," he continues. "On a bike trainer and a regular bike I could be focused and 'in the zone.' But on a bike as I ride outdoors, be it on a trail, paved path, or on the road, I will always be more aware and focused, thus bringing my mindfulness to a higher or greater level than being in a box on a trainer listening to my favorite playlist or podcast."

FOREST BATHING/SHINRIN-YOKU AND MOUNTAIN BIKING

INVITATIONS BEFORE RIDING
Pleasures of Presence

In the tradition of the Standard Sequence, the invitation "Pleasures of Presence" begins each forest bathing walk. It is an effective way to center, calm the monkey mind, and set the tone for the practice. Below is a Pleasures of Presence invitation that is adapted specifically to be done prior to mountain biking.

Invitation: Find some loose soil from the trail on which you are about to ride. Gather the soil in your hands and make your way off the trail to a location without any hiking or cycling traffic. With the soil cupped in your hands, find a place to sit down and close your eyes. Take a few moments to center by breathing slowly and deeply with your eyes closed. After a few deep breaths, bring the soil to your nose and breathe in its fragrance. Notice the scent of the soil as it enters your nostrils, and follow the fragrance as it enters all the way into your lungs. Notice that you are breathing the molecules of your trail all the way into your body. Notice, too, that you are sharing the life force energy with the many microscopic beings that inhabit this soil.

Next, still with closed eyes, notice the way the soil feels in your hands. Notice the temperature of the soil. Is it warm or is it cool to the touch? Notice the texture. Is it rough? Is it smooth? Are there irregularities like small stones or wood? What is the weight of the soil? Does it feel light and airy, or does it feel heavier than you might expect? Is the soil dry, or is it moist to the touch? Finally, allow some, but not all, of the soil to filter through your fingers and fall to the ground. What does this feel like? What does it remind you of or bring to mind as the soil filters through your fingers and falls to the ground?

Now, with your eyes closed, bring your hands up to one of your ears. If you hold the soil to your ears, is there any sound? What if, again, you allow some of the soil to fall to the ground? What sound does it make when it does this? What does it sound like if you crumble some of the soil between your thumb and fingers in the palm of your hand?

Bring your soil, next, up to your lips. What would happen if, with eyes closed, you touched the soil to your lips? What would it feel like on your lips, regarding texture, temperature, and so on? If you are so inclined, consider touching a tiny bit of the soil to your tongue. What does it taste like on the tip of your tongue?

Finally, hold the soil in your cupped hands in front of your face. Imagine that you have no idea what it is that you are holding in your hands, as if someone had handed you this substance while your eyes were closed. Before opening your eyes, imagine what it might look like to see this substance that you have been exploring through your various senses. How much space will it occupy? Will it will be homogeneous or have particles of rock or sticks or even living beings in it? What color will it be? After spending some time in this imaginal state, plan to open your eyes as if you have never seen this substance before. When you are ready, go ahead and open your eyes. Take in the visual experience of the soil that is both a life-giving substance and the foundation of the activity you are about to explore, without which there would be no trail. What do you notice?

What thoughts, emotions, or memories are evoked during your Pleasures of Presence? If possible, share your experience with another person or write it down in a journal as soon as possible.

What's in Motion?

If one is truly seeking to achieve a state of flow during a ride, taking the time to explore the invitation of "What's in Motion?" is a terrific way to accomplish that goal.

Invitation: Take ten minutes to either walk along *very* slowly or even sit in one place, simply noticing what you see in nature that is in motion. Be sure to look up, down, and deep into the underbrush of your trail to fully explore things that are moving. During this invitation, should you become distracted by something else—a sound or another person, for example—just gently bring your awareness back to noticing things that are in motion. You might discover that there is movement right in front of you that otherwise might have been missed had you not taken the time to slow down and look for it. Spend as much time as you feel drawn to spend, simply observing things in motion. The perspective gained from this simple invitation may change your riding experience both immediately and indefinitely. What do you notice? *Does* this change your perspective of your mountain bike trail?

Gazing Up a Tree

This is a visual invitation that brings awareness upward, taking in the magnitude of a tree. It can even be done in an urban setting where there is only one tree. For an activity such as mountain biking, we often spend all our time looking at the ground. Taking some time to "look up" can be very moving and perspective-altering.

Invitation: While lying or sitting on the ground, bring all your awareness to your sense of sight. You are invited to begin by focusing your

eyes on the base of a nearby tree and the ground surrounding the tree, taking in any roots that might be visible that belong to this tree. In fact, explore the ground several feet away from the tree to notice how far out this tree's roots extend. Next, very, very slowly and deliberately, taking about five minutes for the entire experience, trace your eyes up the tree. Notice every detail as you slowly move your gaze up to the very top of the tree. During this invitation, should you be distracted by a sound or another sight, mindfully bring your awareness back to visually climbing up the tree. Afterward, take a moment to make a mental note of your experience. How did this make you feel? Does this resonate with any other aspect of your life? In what way might this affect your mountain biking experience?

Walking Barefoot on the Trail

If it is safe to do so, in an area where one is not likely to be run over by mountain bikers, it can be a very moving experience to walk barefoot on a dirt mountain bike trail. This is also an excellent way to acclimate beginner mountain bikers to the trail in a nonthreatening way. Experienced mountain bikers can expand their relationship to the trail and their surroundings by using this invitation.

Invitation: You are invited to remove your shoes and socks and walk barefoot on the trail. If removing footwear is not desirable, you may sit on the trail and spend quiet time with your hands touching or coming in contact with the trail. Please find a minimally used section of the trail, such as a connector trail, or do this at a time when trail use is minimal. Simply notice what it is like to experience the trail in this tactile way. When you are finished, ask yourself what you noticed. Is there a message for you from this practice? Does this bring back any memories for you? How does that affect you?

INVITATIONS DURING RIDING
Pleasures of Presence

Do you ever find yourself either (a) bored on a long ride and want-
ing to pass the time or (b) struggling to make it up a difficult climb?
Depending upon speed and level of difficulty of the trail, a highly effective strategy is to incorporate the elements of forest bathing.

Invitation: Start by choosing one of the five senses and focusing on
it. For example, notice the sounds around you, perhaps focusing on
the sounds that are farthest away from you. Then notice the sounds
closest to you, perhaps the sound of your heavy breathing! Without
any judgment about the sound of your breathing, just concentrate on
listening to the sound of it. Do you hear natural sounds, such as birds
or insects? What about man-made sounds? Are there sounds made by
your bike? Do you notice recurring sounds or rhythms? Do you hear an
interplay of sounds, back and forth? What other sounds do you notice
as you ride?

Next become aware of your vision, taking in everything that is in
your visual field. What is it like to fully *see* the world from your point of
view on a mountain bike? As you are moving, are you able to see details
of objects that you pass? Notice the blur of trees, plants, landforms, and
other structures as you go by. Notice where your focus on the trail is as
you process your moves. Are you trail scanning or are you focusing right
in front of your bike? If the latter, can you expand your gaze down the
trail and trust your peripheral vision? What else do you see? Are there
animals moving about? Do you see different types of plants and trees?
What does the surface of your trail look like? Do you see lots of color, or
are the colors fairly monochromatic? How far into the distance are you
able to see? What else do you notice via your sense of sight?

North Lake Tahoe, Nevada

The sense of smell can be a surprising way to pass the time, noticing the fragrance of plants, dirt, or other natural or man-made scents. What do you notice from the olfactory sense? Can you smell the fragrance of trees or flowers? Can you smell the soil or other surface of the trail? Can you smell the scent of your clothing or even your bike? Are there any undesirable smells? Do these come from plants or animals or from man? What might be the function of these various smells, whether natural or man-made, welcome or unwelcome? What else do you notice?

Focus, finally, on your sense of touch. What does the air feel like on this day? Is it warm or cold, humid or dry, windy or still? Notice the way the air feels as it blows past your skin as you ride. How does your helmet feel on your head? Where does your clothing contact your body? Do you notice any sources of friction on your skin? If you are wearing gloves, how do they feel on your hands and fingers? How and where do your hands contact the handlebars? What do the brake and gearshift levers feel like? Can you feel your feet in contact with your socks, in contact with your shoes, in contact with the pedals? As you move your bike from side to side, do you notice bike-body separation? Can you imagine becoming one with your bike, as a single unit? What other tactile experiences do you notice?

After your ride or after making it up a difficult hill, reflect upon whether this technique was helpful for you. What else did you notice about the Pleasures of Presence while riding a mountain bike?

What's in Motion?

While riding, notice what (in addition to yourself) in your surroundings is visibly in motion. Focus your attention on only taking in "what's in motion." Be sure to look up, down, and into the distance and notice what is in motion.

This invitation is especially useful during mountain bike racing, as the faster you are riding, the more important it becomes to notice potential hazards (wildlife, humans, vehicles) that may attempt to cross your path. This invitation also helps with processing or trail scanning, because the softer our gaze, the more we can take in.

Invitation: Focusing your eyes twenty feet down the trail, taking in "what's in motion" in a softened gaze, is a highly effective way to improve speed and find your flow. If the desire arises, feel free to stop and look closely at a flower, an insect, or an animal, and observe motion in these beings. Take time to really notice what is in motion. What *do* you see that is in motion when you take the time to notice?

Noticing the Dark

In our day-to-day life, we spend much of our time visually noticing color and light. In mountain biking, however, noticing dark things on the trail (often rocks, tree roots, downed logs, or branches) is very important.

Invitation: While riding, take time to notice other patterns of darkness, focusing your vision on noticing things that are dark over things that are light. Dedicate a portion of your ride to focus on noticing the dark. What patterns do you see? What do we miss when we focus only on the light?

Body Scan

It is easy to focus on discomfort during a physical activity, particularly during endurance sports. A body scan can help to ease sore muscles and joints. Take a moment, while continuing to ride, to scan your body, doing a little body awareness and even progressive muscle relaxation, as you go.

Invitation: Start at the top of your head and notice the feeling of your hair and scalp. Notice the way your helmet feels on top of your head. Avoid making judgments about the way your body feels—just notice. Move your scalp by raising and lowering your eyebrows and feel your helmet move back and forth. Next, notice your forehead. Scrunch it up and release it. Squeeze your eyes shut tightly for a second, and then notice your eyelids relax. Next, scrunch and release your nose, puff up and relax your cheeks, stick your tongue out, and stretch and contort your mouth a few times. Feel the relaxation take over your face and head, and notice the air moving past your face. Move your head from side to side, back and forth, and up and down a few times.

Slickrock Trails, Moab, Utah

North Lake Tahoe, Nevada

Then move on to your arms. While riding, straighten and bend your arms a few times. Let one arm dangle, reach backward, and move in a big circle, returning to the handlebars. Repeat this sequence with the other arm. Wiggle your fingers a few times. Notice the blood filling your hands when they hang downward, and notice any numbness that is relieved by moving your arms. Allow your arms to feel soft and supple, and notice the wind moving over your entire upper extremities. Next, arch your back forward and backward a few times. Take some deep breaths and allow your chest to expand. Notice the space behind your heart and allow it to expand with space and energy. Move your abdomen in and out.

Do what you can to flex and extend your lower extremities. If stopping is an option, stretching the quads, hamstrings, adductors, and abductors is a great idea. If stopping is not an option, perform micro-stretches as you can. In other words, wiggle your feet within your shoes, shift your pelvis side-to-side and front-to-back, or stretch an arm outward as you are able. Notice the muscles in your thighs as they go through the rhythm of pedaling you forward. Notice the muscles in your hamstrings, your shins, your calves. Notice the movements in your hip joints, knee joints, and ankle joints. Become lost for a moment in the rhythm of these movements. Notice the air passing over your lower extremities as you ride. Finally, notice the temperature, moisture, scent, and wind speed of the air as it passes your body. Notice the sensations as you breathe the air, shared by all the plants and animals in your midst, into the body. Imagine the oxygen in this shared air nourishing your muscles and organs, allowing you the gift of riding this ride. How does this make you feel?

Of My Life

One of my favorite standard ANFT invitations is "Of My Life." Depending upon the situation, this invitation can add levity after moments of deep introspection. Paradoxically, it can surprise forest bathers, too, with moments of insight.

Invitation: As you are riding, think the words "of my life." Then, as you notice items along the trail, say the name of the item (out loud, ideally!), followed by the words "of my life." For example, if you see tree roots, you might say "the roots of my life." If you see a cobweb, you might say "the cobweb of my life." Go on with "the path of my life," and so on. What were some of your favorite "of my life" phrases? How did you react to them? Did any thoughts arise from this invitation?

INVITATIONS AFTER RIDING
Sit Spot

Following your mountain bike adventure, what better way to cool down than to enjoy a Sit Spot? Although there is no expectation to do or contemplate anything in particular during Sit Spot, sometimes it is nice to pose a question to yourself. You might ask yourself in what way you feel capable as a mountain biker and then choose to share that, in some way, with the forest. You might then ask the forest to help you share gratitude for that ability. Take time to simply notice any physical, mental, and emotional sensations in the body during Sit Spot, and take in your surroundings. What do you notice? Journaling following Sit Spot is a terrific way to culminate this practice and to solidify the experience.

Gratitude Altar

After riding, the invitation "Gratitude Altar" is a powerful way to connect your mind-body experience to your natural surroundings and to your sport.

Invitation: Take a moment to stop, expand your gaze, and notice something from your mountain bike trail that "speaks" to you in some way or that elicits a sense of gratitude. Perhaps a rock, a pinecone, a feather, or a leaf or flower commands your attention. Pick up a few of these items and step over to a safe and quiet area off the trail. Next, find an item related to mountain biking, such as your helmet, gloves, water bottle, or even your bike itself. Arrange the biking items and the natural items that you have collected in a way that seems fitting, and step back to admire your "still-life" work of art. Ask yourself what made you choose the items you brought to your arrangement—do they evoke a memory of a person, place, or earlier

time? What emotions come forward? In what way does your work of art evoke a sense of gratitude? And, finally, how do the elements from the natural world intertwine or interrelate with the man-made items from mountain biking? What do you notice? What do you take away from this? Consider writing or journaling about this experience.

Horseshoe Canyon, Driggs, Idaho

TEA CEREMONY: BROADLEAF PLANTAIN

The *shinrin-yoku* mountain biking excursion is made complete by ending with the traditional tea ceremony. I can not think of a more appropriate tea plant for a post-ride ceremony.

One of the most abundantly available edible and medicinal plants is the common or broadleaf plantain (*Plantago major*). One can find this plant at trailheads, in ditches, in lawns, and in disturbed areas (e.g., trails!). It's everywhere. Originally native to Europe and northern and central Asia, this plant has been naturalized all over the world. Often considered a weed, plantain is a highly useful and completely safe herb to use medicinally. Please see the sidebar in this chapter for one of the best uses for plantain: as a poultice to stop bleeding or to treat insect bites and stings. This is a convenient tip for the mountain biking community!

When foraging for this plant, notice that it has broad, rounded, oval leaves, measuring five to twenty centimeters long and four to nine centimeters wide. Leaves tend to have between five and nine deep, conspicuous veins. Its flowers, present in midsummer, are narrow green spikes, often with purple anthers when in full bloom.

The entire plant is edible and may be used in salads and stews. For a tea ceremony, gather younger leaves that are off the trail, away from foot/bike/animal/vehicle traffic. Older leaves tend to be more fibrous, so look for soft, young, smaller leaves.

Allow your tea to steep for at least five minutes, and then prepare to enjoy. Remember to offer a cup of your tea back to the earth, as part of the traditional ceremony. Prior to taking your first sip, pause to close your eyes and take a sniff of your tea. What ailments does it seem this tea might be useful for?

Plant Wisdom: Nature's First-Aid Remedy— Broadleaf Plantain

You crash your bike on some rocks and blood is everywhere. While collecting yourself, you get eaten alive by mosquitoes. It never fails that accidents happen, the first-aid kit is at the trailhead, and some ancient wisdom might come in handy. Common broadleaf plantain, or *Plantago major*, is your answer for minor wounds, stings, and bites.

Plantain is ubiquitous worldwide along trails, meadows, parking lots, ditches, sidewalks—you name it. Recognize it by its broad, oval leaves spreading close to the ground, with its tall, slender spires of green seeds and purplish flowers.

Gather a small handful of these leaves (preferably untrampled), stick them in your mouth, and chew them up . . . but don't swallow! Apply this "spit poultice" directly to the wound or bite. If possible, wrap a cloth over the poultice to keep the herbs in place. Leave in place for thirty to forty-five minutes.

Plantain is said to have drawing properties that wick foreign substances from the skin, even helping to bring a deep splinter to the surface. It is known to have styptic properties that help blood to clot, as well as have antimicrobial and anti-inflammatory actions.

If you thought your tea might be soothing to injured or inflamed tissues, you would be correct. Its compounds have been studied and found to contain therapeutic flavonoids, allantoin, and ursolic acid, among others. Research has confirmed that plantain has anti-inflammatory, wound-healing, analgesic, antioxidant, and even antibiotic properties.

In tea form, plantain is used to soothe inflamed internal tissues, such as stomach ulcers and inflammatory bowel disorders. It is used as a diuretic and as an expectorant for coughs. It has been found to be high in calcium and vitamins A, C, and K. This lends credence to its use for treating scrapes and cuts, as vitamin K is necessary for clot formation.

One might be surprised to learn that the seeds from a cultivated form of plantain, called *P. psyllium*, are used as a bulk laxative in such

The Science of Nature: Health Effects That Last!

Did you know that Dr. Qing Li, in Japan, has studied the effect of time spent in nature on our immune system's natural killer (NK) cells? He has found that these NK cells, which fight off and kill unhealthy cells in the body such as tumor cells and those infected with viruses, actually increase in number and are more active after a forest bathing trip lasting three days and two nights. Specifically, he found that NK cell numbers rose by 50 percent and that their activity rose by 53 percent. Even more striking is the fact that this rise and activity of NK cells remained elevated for *thirty* days after a three-day forest bathing trip! (Li et al. 2008)

commercial preparations as Metamucil. Needless to say, the seeds of the common plantain produce a similar effect.

During the tea ceremony, take time to appreciate the land on which you have ridden. Reflect upon the earliest human inhabitants of this land, and mentally or verbally express your gratitude to these people for tending the land. If you know the names of the Native tribes of the area, acknowledge them by name. If you do not know this information, make a pledge to yourself to learn it. Recognize that land acknowledgment is a simple way to honor the Native population, anywhere in the world.

As you enjoy your plantain tea, take a moment to appreciate your senses of taste and smell and to appreciate the fact that, via this tea ceremony, you are fully and intentionally taking the forest into your body. Take a moment to acknowledge the medicinal properties of the common plantain, this ubiquitous "weed" that has so much to offer. Also take a moment to consider the analogy of plantain as a wound healer and plantain's tendency to grow in "disturbed" areas. Is there a broader purpose for this healing plant?

In Closing

At around the twenty-seven-mile mark of the forty-five-mile version of the Lutsen 99er mountain bike race (inappropriately named the Lutsen *39*er), a pretty decent climb took place. I was riding by myself on Lutsen Mountain, while my husband Joe was tackling the 99er. It seemed that there was less collegiality among riders in this race, compared to others, so that left plenty of time—all alone in my head—to concentrate on the misery of climbing some of these hills. At least during the 1,000-foot climb in the first six miles of the race, there had been onlookers cheering us on. But by mile 27, there were literally crickets.

As I was starting to wonder why I signed up for this, I was treated to an amazing blast of pine fragrance. It was like a gift to behold this scent from my very favorite tree—the timing *must* have been divinely orchestrated. I focused on the pine fragrance, drawing it in and out of

my lungs with each heaving breath, as if I had to take it all in before it was gone. In just a moment, my breathing became less labored, as I focused on the pine scent as opposed to my doom and gloom. I looked up from the rocky trail to take in the sight of my magnificent benefactors: white pine, I realized.

My heart was filled with awe as I took in the sight of these towering beings, which had completely enveloped our trail. They gave me shade, they gave me a beautiful sight to distract me from staring at the trail, and they gave me this exquisite fragrance. I focused on all of these gifts, one by one, reveling in the sensory explosion of it all. I was overcome with a sense of gratitude for the splendor of nature, for the opportunity to ride in this race, and for my able body. And just like that, I found myself gearing up . . . at the *summit*.

CLIMBING

"Take!" I shouted down to the belayer. My fingers were completely frozen and numb. I could barely hold on to my ice axes. My knees were bruised and my arms were trembling with fatigue. It was January and I was clinging to the side of a frozen grain silo on a farm in northeast Iowa, about seventy feet from the ground. I was spent, but it was my third attempt at scaling this thing. Oh my *God*, I wanted to give up. But I really, *really* was determined to make it to the top. I had a glimmer of a thought at how crazy we Iowans are that we would freeze an old silo for ice climbing, but when you are flatlanders you do what you must!

As I perched there, I thought of how nice it would be to rappel down and go inside the climbing lodge to warm up. And then I remembered the sense of accomplishment I felt after finishing other physically demanding challenges; some of those scenarios ran through my mind. I realized that I wanted *that* more than a cup of hot chocolate and a sense of frustration, followed by the self-flagellation that I knew would ensue. I looked down at the tiny people on the ground and realized how high I had already climbed. I looked up, and the last ten feet still looked remarkably far away.

The thought then occurred to me that I was going to get to the top of this silo, whether it was today or another day. If not today, I would have to *re-climb* the entire seventy feet again. In that case, I might as

well dig deep and finish that last remaining ten feet *today*. And that is exactly what I did. I repeated "Dig. Deep." with every movement of every limb until I was at the top.

The exhilaration of reaching the top seems to universally draw people to climbing. It is an inherent human trait to reach the outer limits of our physical boundaries, whether they are up, down, or across bodies of water, yet there seems to be something uniquely compelling about climbing *up*. But what else is it? Is there something, also, about the symbolism of the achievement?

To quote Nietzsche: "In the mountain of truth, one never climbs in vain, you either reach a higher step today or exercise your strength to climb higher tomorrow." Substitute other virtues for "truth" (courage, justice, faith, hope, temperance, and others), and "digging deep" may mean different things to different people on any given day. These were the life lessons that revealed themselves to me, that cold day on the silo.

History and Stewardship

Humans have been climbing rocks and mountains for as long as there have been humans, rocks, and mountains. Reasons for climbing have included necessity (exploration, war, and, simply, to get from place to place) and also, as George Mallory said of his reason to climb Mount Everest, simply "because it is there." A perusal through the history of mountaineering shows references to monumental climbs as far back as the late 1400s, but it was not until the 1800s that "modern" equipment in the form of ropes, ice axes, and crude crampons was used.

Fast-forward to the early 1900s, when the concept of "artificial aid," including early carabiners, bolts, and pitons, came into existence. Climbing as a sport is believed to have originated simultaneously in various regions in Europe in the late nineteenth century and has subsequently spread to all corners of the globe. Climbing today has taken on a number of different forms including sport climbing, traditional (or "trad") climbing, toprope climbing, free solo climbing, aid climbing, and bouldering, details of which are beyond the scope of this book.

As with all sports, there are national and international organizations dedicated to the practice and regulation of climbing and mountaineering, as well as to the conservation of the mountains, rock formations, and surrounding natural spaces that climbers hope to preserve.

Internationally, the UIAA is an organization of climbers and alpinists founded in Chamonix, France, in 1932 as the Union Internationale des Associations d'Alpinisme, currently known in the United States as the International Climbing and Mountaineering Federation (www.theuiaa .org). The original mission of this organization was to be in charge of "study and solution of all problems regarding mountaineering." In addition to developing standards of safety for climbing equipment, one of its accomplishments was the designation in 1967 of the UIAA international scale of climbing difficulty. To this day, UIAA maintains an investment in environmentalism. In 1982 UIAA announced a call to action against the degradation of mountains, known as the Kathmandu Declaration, and in 2009 approved the Mountain Ethics Declaration, which, according to its website, is "a code for mountaineering values, spelling out sportsmanship ethics and respect for cultures and the environment."

To promote and preserve the climbing way of life, the American Alpine Club (AAC) has been in existence in the United States since 1902, with wildlife preservation champion John Muir serving as its second president. The website (https://americanalpineclub.org) reads, "Starting with Muir, the club has held a central role in environmental conservation, developing relationships with the U.S. Forest Service and National Park Service to balance land use with preservation needs in addressing ethics, access, wilderness management, registration, huts, and roads."

Mindfulness in Rock Climbing

There are not many pursuits that I can think of that are more mindful than climbing. When one's life is hanging (literally) from a rope or a ledge, an intensity of focus is required, and getting into the zone becomes a life-sustaining necessity. Perhaps this is one reason climbers are drawn to the sport, as a way to flee the challenges and stresses of everyday life.

FOREST BATHING/SHINRIN-YOKU AND ROCK CLIMBING

INVITATIONS BEFORE CLIMBING
Pleasures of Presence

Staring up a wall you are about to climb can be a bit unnerving. Taking a moment to ground yourself and settle into the moment not only calms the nerves, but is also a good tool to add to the safety check. When you begin a climb in a more mindful state, you are less likely to make errors and forget things. The "Pleasures of Presence" invitation is just the trick for this.

Invitation: Find a place where you can comfortably sit, that is close enough to the wall or boulder that you can reach out and touch it. If you wish, you may sit with your back against the wall. Begin by closing your eyes and taking a few slow, deep breaths, then note the name of the place in which you are sitting and, if applicable, the name of the wall you are preparing to climb. Acknowledge the tribes of people who first inhabited this area, by name if possible. Imagine, for a moment, the way people hundreds of years ago may have used this space. How might the topography have factored into their daily lives? How long have people climbed this wall, these mountains,

Plant Wisdom: Sage vs. Sagebrush

Are sage and sagebrush the same thing? When I think of outdoor climbing in the United States, I envision the enormous rocky masterpieces out west. I picture the landscape of many of these areas as dotted with sagebrush, as well as with various types of sage. It might surprise people to learn that although they all have aromatic, dusty white-green leaves, sage and sagebrush do not belong to the same family.

Members of the sage, or *Salvia*, plant genus are members of the larger mint (Lamiaceae) family. A fun and easy-to-remember fact about mints is that all members of this family have a square-shaped stem. Twirl a stalk between your fingers, and you will never forget the four-sided shape of mint-family stems. In addition to white and culinary sage, the mint family also includes clary sage, spearmint, peppermint, lemon balm, catnip (or catmint), and oregano.

Sagebrush (also known as sagewort), on the other hand, belongs to the genus *Artemisia*, of the family Asteraceae, the same family as daisy, dandelion, and ragweed. These plants do not have four-sided stems. The Latin name *Artemisia tridentata* provides a second clue distinguishing it from sage: Sagebrush's leaves have three teeth at their tips (*tri* meaning "three," and *dentata* meaning "toothed").

The distribution of sagebrush (*Artemisia tridentata*) in the United States includes all of Nevada (in fact, it is their state flower), much of the eastern halves of Oregon and Washington, southern Idaho, and most of Wyoming and Montana, as well as scattered areas in Utah, western Colorado, northern Arizona and New Mexico, and southern California. In contrast, white sage (*Salvia apiana*) grows predominantly in southern California and Baja California, and culinary sage (*Salvia officinalis*) can be found in much of eastern Canada and the United States, with the exception of a wide swath through the Plains states in the center of the country.

The powerful plant medicine of the salvias has been known for hundreds of years. It is interesting to note that the English word *sage* means a person of wisdom. The Latin word, *salvia*, shares the root word of *salvation* and is derived from the Latin root word *salvere*, meaning "to heal." The burning of dried white sage leaves is used by various Pacific Native American tribes in purification or smudging

rituals, meant to clear negative energy. Besides being used in cook-
ing, culinary sage (or simply "sage") is used for the treatment of sore
throat, coughs, and colds; for excessive sweating (including meno-
pausal hot flashes); and even to enhance memory.

Sagebrush leaves have been used medicinally for many of the same
purposes as sage throughout history. A publication even documents
the use of powdered sagebrush for the treatment of athlete's foot
(Camazine 1980).

A note of caution: These *Artemisia* and *Salvia* species all contain
compounds called "thujones." It has been established that thujones
act as antagonists to GABA receptors in the body and have been implicated in causing seizures (Höld et al. 2000). In the amounts of sage
ingested in culinary use, seizures have not been reported; however,
ingesting large amounts of any of these plants for medicinal use, or
ingesting their essential oils, can have toxic results.

The next time you come across a sage-like plant, twirl a stalk
between your fingers, examine the leaves, close your eyes, take a
whiff, and send forth some gratitude for these wise old healing herbs.

A landscape of sagebrush and juniper

Now an architect and dad, David Sharratt dedicated a decade of his life to climbing, establishing first ascents on remote alpine peaks around the globe and on boulders and cliffs in his stomping grounds of New England and western North Carolina. David and his wife Anna, also a climber, sat down to discuss the Zen of climbing and the role that nature plays in attaining it.

David said, "Climbing is all about being 100 percent focused on the details of your position in the environment. This ranges from the small scale to the large scale. For example, how you understand the complexity of the geometries of the handholds and how they relate to your center of mass on an overhanging boulder. Or calculating time and distance related to the approach of an incoming storm while climbing on a summit or exposed ridge. Climbing in the mountains in particular demands an unrelenting attention to your personal physical state and a sometimes dangerously capricious environment."

I asked David how climbing in nature is different from indoor climbing, in terms of achieving mindfulness. He replied, "It's integral and fundamentally what draws many climbers to the sport. On a basic level, challenge and exercise outdoors are healthy and wonderful

these boulders? What significance might this wall have had for indigenous peoples?

Consider, for a moment, the current way in which humans interact with this wall, this space. Are the actions of humans causing an impact, either positively or negatively? How does that make you feel? Then things. For me, climbing was always an excuse to explore beautiful places. In a way, climbing is a practice for better understanding and appreciating wild places, the kind of understanding you can only get from pushing yourself."

I also asked David whether he notices that the sights, sounds, and smells of nature factor into his ability to "get in the zone" while climbing. "Yes," he said, "although somewhat inadvertently. Most of my hardest ascents have followed moments when I step back and really soak something from nature in—be it the golden evening light, birdsong, a breeze, or an inspiring view." He continued, "The intense focus and effort that hard climbing—and by hard climbing, I mean at your absolute limit—demands, when you are doing it well—and by doing it well, I mean you have a feeling of being in flow—you step out of yourself and it's a bit primal."

I think he minimizes the "primal" part, as I reflect upon David's words. I sense that it is this "primal" thing that gets to the heart of what forest bathing is all about. It seems to run deep within all of us to run, walk, and climb fully immersed and absorbed in connection with nature.

imagine, in your mind's eye, the beings in the more-than-human world that make this place their home. In what way does this wall provide food or shelter for these plant and animal beings? How do you suppose that changes with the time of day or with the seasons?

Next, bring your awareness back to your breathing, taking some deeper breaths in and out, making a conscious effort to slow your exhalation. You may even wish to count to four as you inhale, and count to four as you exhale. Over the next few breaths, continue to breathe in for the count of four, but exhale for a count of six. Next, breathe in for four, out for eight. Do this a few more times and note your heart rate begin to settle.

As you breathe, notice first the scent of the air around you. What do you smell? Do you smell any plants or flowers nearby? What else do you notice? If you turn so that you are facing the wall, what does *it* smell like? How would you describe that scent? Do you detect moisture in the air coming off the rock, or does the air feel dry as it enters your nasal passages? What does the smell of the wall remind you of?

Now, turn your attention to your ears. What sounds do you hear? Can you begin to separate these sounds into sounds that are near and sounds that are far away? Can you separate the sounds by direction? If you direct your attention toward the wall, do you notice any sounds coming from the wall? If not, what if you cup your hand around your ear and point it toward the wall? Does this change anything? Move your head so that your ear is just a few inches from the wall. What do you hear? If you actually touch your ear to the wall, now what? Is it completely silent? Do you hear any signs of animal, plant, or insect movement? If you bring your hand to the wall near your ear, what does it sound like if you scratch the wall with your fingers or fingernails? How about if you use your knuckles to knock on the wall? What does that sound like? Take a moment to imagine drawing all of these sounds into your body.

As you are sitting next to your wall with eyes closed, think about your sense of taste. Perhaps within your mouth you can still taste a bit of your last meal or snack. Open your mouth slightly and notice whether you can actually taste the air around you on your tongue. Feel free to even stick your tongue out and notice the taste of the air. If you're feeling up to it, you might even decide to taste the wall . . . but use your own discretion! What are you noticing about these tastes?

Next, notice the presence of your body in this space. Feel the sensation of your body touching the ground. If you are leaning up against the rock, feel the points at which your body is in contact with it. How does the size of your body compare with the natural elements around you? With eyes closed, take one or both hands and place them on the wall or boulder. What does it feel like? Does it evoke any memories? What is the texture of the wall? Is it smooth or rough? Is there any gritty particulate matter on it? Is it clear of plant material, or do you feel plants or moss? What do those things feel like? Is the wall dry, or does it have any moisture? And, next, what do you notice about the temperature of the rock? How does it compare with the temperature of the air? If you press your cheek up to the wall, how does that change the tactile experience? Imagine, for a moment, the weight of the wall. Can you begin to imagine how much it weighs? Do any emotions arise from connecting with the wall in this way? What else do you notice from a proprioceptive or tactile perspective?

Finally, begin to prepare to open your eyes. As you sit next to the wall, with eyes still closed, see if you can carefully turn so that you are facing it. You may even wish to shift your weight back onto your elbows, or even to lie back (if space allows and you can do this safely with eyes closed or with lowered gaze). Once you are situated, still with eyes closed, prepare to take in your entire field of vision with a softened gaze. Give yourself a count of three, and then open your eyes to take in the entire expanse of your wall, boulder, or mountain. Take it all in for as long as you wish.

When you feel you have completed your journey through the Pleasures of Presence, return your awareness to your surroundings. What were some of the things you noticed during this sensory experience? Discuss with a partner, journal, or jot some notes about any observations, memories, or revelations that may have arisen.

What's in Motion?

A terrific way to survey a wall prior to climbing is to complete the invitation "What's in Motion?" As with Pleasures of Presence, this practice generates mindfulness as well as an awareness of one's surroundings.

Invitation: Start by setting a timer for ten to twenty minutes, and begin in a standing position. Walking slowly, either parallel to the base of the wall or out on the trail leading up to the wall, visually notice what you can see that is moving. Take in the movement of plants, animals, birds, insects, and anything else that you notice, from the largest to the smallest of movements. Feel free to stop for as long as you like if something catches your eye. You may even choose to sit, squat, or stand in one place for the entire duration if a moving object captures your interest. Should your mind wander from the task of looking at things that are in motion, gently bring it back.

At the completion of your invitation, ask yourself what you noticed. Journal, write some notes, or share your observations with a partner.

Visual Ascent

Climbers often use visualization techniques to mentally rehearse a route prior to setting out, so this invitation takes this practice literally.

Herbal Insight: The Prickly Pear Cactus

Did you know that the prickly pear cactus (*Opuntia* spp.) is full of healing properties? Found in desert climates all over the southwestern United States and in many arid regions of the world, the inner pulp of this plant has been used historically to fight scurvy (caused by vitamin C deficiency) and to reduce blood sugar in non-insulin-dependent diabetes. As a practical measure for outdoor enthusiasts, the pulp may be used as a sunscreen as well as an anti-inflammatory poultice for wounds, burns, and sprains. Watch out for the sharp spines, but share some appreciation for these invaluable succulents the next time you pass one by.

Invitation: Lying on your back facing the climbing route, take five minutes—by the clock—to visually ascend the wall. To do this, fix your gaze on the ground at the base of the route and ever-so-slowly work your way up the wall, visually taking in every minute detail in the process. As with "What's in Motion?," if your gaze becomes distracted, gently remind yourself to return to the place at which you lost focus. Avoid the temptation to move your gaze too quickly to the top of the wall; instead, attempt to use the entire five minutes to make it to the top. When you visually reach the top, consider what you observed along the route. What are you noticing? How might this affect your climb?

INVITATIONS DURING CLIMBING
Pleasures of Presence

The physical and mental intensity of climbing can be very taxing to the body and mind. In order to alleviate some of the strain, the Pleasures of Presence can be incorporated very effectively. One way to do this is to decide on a set duration during which to focus on a particular type of sensory input. For example, you might choose to focus on the sense of touch for an entire pitch. Or you might focus on the sense of sight for a period of time by the clock.

Invitation: As you focus on sight, notice areas that are dark versus areas that are light. Does darkness correspond to moisture or a particular variation in texture? Are there areas on the wall that are reflective or shiny? Are these reflections seen throughout the rock or only in certain areas? What colors do you notice? If you squint your eyes, can you determine the visual features that allow you to see hand- and footholds? On what side of these holds do shadows fall? What do you notice about the motions of your limbs as you climb? Are they smooth and fluid or interrupted and choppy? Is there other motion on the wall besides your body, or is there generalized stillness?

After your visual exploration, begin noticing your sense of touch. As you climb, how many points of contact are there between your body and the wall at any given moment? What does it feel like to use your body in this way? What does it feel like to touch the wall with your hands and fingers? Is the wall cold, or is it warmer than your body temperature? Does this change with certain positions on the wall, or does the temperature remain constant? What textures do you notice? What does the texture of chalk feel like compared to the texture of the wall? How is this texture similar to or different from other textures on which you have climbed, such as different types of rock . . . maybe ice? How do your feet register their sensations of the wall, and how do different hand, finger, and foot positions feel against the wall? How does it feel to use your knees and hips against the wall? While you are noticing these body parts, how do they feel internally? How is your grip? Are you holding unnecessary tension or over-gripping? Are you using your limbs and muscles efficiently, or are you making the work unnecessarily difficult? How can you use body awareness to make life easier for yourself as you climb?

Next, consider the sounds of climbing. Notice, first, the sounds of your breathing. Is your breathing labored or relaxed? Without judging it, are you able to smooth out your breathing? Can you fall into a rhythm with your breathing and with the sounds of your body movements as you climb? What else do you hear? What does it sound like when your hands and feet come into contact with the wall? What sounds does your gear make as you move: the rope, hardware, chalk bag? Have you ever noticed those sounds before? What sounds of nature can you hear? What if you spend a certain amount of time simply listening for sounds of nature as you climb?

Finally, breathe in through your nose and take in the scents of climbing. What does the wall *smell* like? Does the scent remind you of other climbing experiences? Does it remind you of anything else? In addition to the wall itself, are there other fragrances that you notice? Can you smell any plants, trees, or flowers? What does the air smell like? What other scents do you notice?

Make a mental note of your sights, sounds, smells, tactile sensations, and proprioceptive observations during your climb. Afterward, take a moment to reflect upon these things and to journal a bit.

What's in Motion?

It is easy to believe that a wall, mountain, or boulder is a static entity, devoid of motion, in and of itself. If you take the time to inspect, however, you will find your climbing wall to be teeming with life.

Invitation: As you climb, invite yourself to notice signs of life in "What's in Motion?" You may need to look at the wall differently: investigate cracks, scan sideways across the face of the wall, look up. Simply search for signs of motion as you climb. Are you surprised at what *is* in motion on the wall? What do you notice?

How Is This Like That?

Often when I spend contemplative time in nature, I play a little game that I call "How Is *This* Like *That*?" As I walk/run/paddle/climb, I will see what items in nature catch my eye and pique my curiosity. Then I will ask myself how this item that I am looking at is, in some way, similar to something else in my life. Perhaps it will create an analogy or a metaphor to a question I have been asking or a problem I have been dealing with.

My favorite example occurred while running during the time that I was dealing with significant physician burnout. I saw a large black feather stuck in a big, fat, thorny thistle right in the middle of my path. You can imagine what that symbolized to me, and the rest, as they say, is history.

Invitation: As you climb, this invitation is one that can easily be implemented. Perhaps even the act of climbing (or reaching the top) is, in some way, analogous to another aspect of your life. Perhaps there is something else, as you scan your surroundings and notice the more-than-human world, that will pique your curiosity and somehow provide an answer. What do you notice? How *is* this like that?

Make Like a Spider

Have you ever watched a spider, insect, or small animal scale a wall, seeming to defy gravity? Sometimes it behooves us larger, gangly animals to make like a spider as we work to climb a wall. Although we cannot grow additional limbs, we can imitate these smaller beings as we climb.

Invitation: See if you can spot an insect, spider, or mammal scrambling up the wall as you climb. Notice the way it uses its limbs and body to efficiently propel itself. If you could step back from the wall and look at yourself, what changes could you make to your posture, your limb movement, or the length of your reach to be more like these agile creatures? Attempt to make a change, first, with your body position. Are you sticking out awkwardly from the wall, or are you flat against the wall? Which is more like a spider? Check your lower limbs. Are your leg movements nimble like a spider? How about your arms and hands? Do you grasp with spiderlike dexterity? What is it like to "make like a spider" as you climb?

Introduce Yourself

Climbing is one of those activities where there is often quite a bit of alone time. Rather than talking to yourself (although I often do!), talk to the wall. Introduce yourself. Allow me to explain:

> During my forest therapy guide practicum, we were required to use an invitation called "Introduction to the Forest" in at least two of our certification walks. Since it was a required invitation, I had to include it to become certified. One of our goals as forest therapy guides is to push our participants to find the "edge"—that place where we are slightly outside our comfort zone. For me, as a guide, "Introduction to the Forest" reached that edge. I found, though, that when I finally tried it, it was one of the invitations that offered an especially magical and often profoundly meaningful experience to forest bathers.

Invitation: As you climb, decide that you will introduce yourself to the wall. Put your inhibitions aside, knowing that no one else will hear you, and out loud—even if only in a whisper—introduce yourself. There are various different ways that you might do this. You might state your name, where you live, what you do, in the same way you would introduce yourself at a dinner party. You might also introduce yourself by sharing some of your family's lineage. Where did your people come from? How many generations of grandparents in your lineage can you name and share with the wall?

You might even share with the wall a question you have been asking and for which you are seeking answers. Consider, for this day and this climb, that the wall may respond to you. Listen carefully with all of your senses and notice whether you hear, see, feel, or smell something that forms an answer. Does the wall respond in some way with *its* lineage? What would this place say to you, if it knew that you would listen? Do any answers materialize? Remember to record or journal about this experience when you are back on solid ground.

Solid as a Rock

"Solid as a rock."

"Rock of ages."

"Their marriage was rocky."

We use rock metaphors all the time. What other metaphors come to mind as you climb?

Invitation: Think of other climbing-related metaphors, phrases, analogies, similes, and symbolism as you climb. Think of the wall's attributes, such as a crack ("cracking up," "she's starting to crack") or the summit ("false summits"). Think of other rock-related phrases. Consider your gear ("learning the ropes," "hanging by a rope"), and so on. What else do you come up with? Do your ideas reflect aspects of your life in some way?

Hug a Tree, Hug a Mountain

Tactile experiences can forever change one's relationship with nature. As mocked and cliché as "tree hugging" is, I have found that there really is nothing like it. There is also nothing more grounding (energetically, physically, and mentally) than spending time clinging to the side of a mountain. So why not embrace it . . . literally?

Invitation: As you climb, pay attention to all of the points of contact between your body and the wall. You may wish to start at your feet and notice the tactile sensation of your toes and feet as you climb. Notice the sensations of pressure, texture, temperature, and anything else you can feel. Move up the body, noticing your lower legs, knees, hips, and

so on, all the way up to your chest and arms. Finally, see if you can notice all of these points simultaneously. What is that like? Then (why not?), when an opportune moment arrives, take a break and hug the mountain! Notice how it feels to do so.

INVITATIONS AFTER CLIMBING
Visual Ascent (Reprise)

Do you take time to revel in your successes, or do you tend to rush off in search of the next project, challenge, or goal? To celebrate the accomplishment of a climbing goal, allow yourself the enjoyment of repeating the visual ascent *afterward*. Indulge in some joy, and honor yourself for a moment.

Invitation: As with the pre-climbing invitation, lie on the ground facing the wall. Slowly follow the route you took from the base to the top, over the course of about five minutes. Is your perspective different this time? Are there things you notice after climbing that you missed the first time around? How do you feel, emotionally, compared to the pre-climb visual ascent? Have you learned new information since the last time? Did the pre-climb visual ascent affect your climb in any way? How so? What else do you notice? Journaling or discussing the experience will help to solidify your memory and may even enhance personal growth.

Sit Spot

The "Visual Ascent" invitation (above) may morph directly into Sit Spot. Take twenty minutes (again, by the clock) to simply sit and absorb your natural surroundings. There is no requirement to specifically appreciate any of the senses, other than to just observe whatever commands your attention. Notice what happens during Sit Spot, both internally and in your surroundings. Notice what happens to the living beings during the time that you sit with them, and take the time to journal or jot notes about your experience when you are finished.

TEA CEREMONY: DANDELION

It seems that most people can identify the dandelion plant (*Taraxacum officinale*). In fact, it seems that many Americans are determined to extinguish this plant from the face of the earth, considering it a pesky weed. Many would likely be surprised to learn that dandelion is valuable as a medicinal herb. Dandelion belongs to the plant family Asteraceae and, as most people are aware, has many small yellow flowers, or florets, combined into the recognizable composite flower head.

For the post-climbing tea ceremony, dandelion is an excellent option, as it is often found near trails and trailheads, and even in the cracks of rock walls. Choose plants that are a bit away from the trail, which are less likely to have been trampled upon, driven on, or visited by trail dogs. Dandelion is a simple choice, as all of the aboveground (or "aerial") parts—flowers, leaves, stems—as well as the roots are edible. Simply gather some aerial parts, fill your tea vessel, add nearly

boiling water, and steep for five minutes. Medicinally, it has long been known that dandelion offers diuretic effects. In other words, consuming dandelion can assist with excess fluid retention by increasing the output of urine. Pharmaceutical diuretics are commonly used for people who have ankle swelling from venous insufficiency and for people with high blood pressure and heart failure.

Additionally, dandelion is known as an herbal "bitter." This category of herbs is used to aid digestion, relieving bloating and fullness after a meal and helping guide the process of moving food through the digestive system. Many cultures use digestive bitters after every meal; fennel, licorice, anise, peppermint, chamomile, and ginger (among others) all fall into this category.

Another of dandelion's therapeutic properties is that it serves as an anti-inflammatory. Knowing that inflammation is a common occurrence after any physical exertion makes dandelion tea an excellent post-activity beverage.

The word *dandelion* is derived from the French *dent de lion*, meaning "lion's tooth," after the coarsely toothed leaves of the plant. It is amusing to note that dandelion has the English folk name "piss-a-bed" and the French nickname *pissenlit*, both for its diuretic effects. Italians refer to the plant as *pisacan*, meaning "dog pisses," due to its growth alongside streets and sidewalks!

There is a relative contraindication (though little scientific evidence) of using dandelion during pregnancy and breastfeeding, and those with allergies to ragweed may react to it. In large quantities there are potential drug interactions with quinolone antibiotics, lithium, potassium-sparing diuretics, and medications that are metabolized by the cytochrome P450 1A2 (or CYP1A2) pathway. Specifically, dandelion can downregulate CYP1A2, therefore increasing the effect of

The Science of Nature: A New Source of Pain Relief

A Korean study of sixty-one individuals with chronic widespread pain showed that those who participated in a two-day forest therapy program reported significant reduction in pain and depression, as well as increased quality of life, compared with controls.

They also found that participants in the forest therapy group, as compared to the control group, showed positive physiological changes. This was evidenced by a significant increase in heart rate variability, as well as an increase in natural killer (NK) cell activity, which is a measure of immune system competence (Han 2016).

In the era of opioid overuse, perhaps forest therapy can be considered a cost-effective integrative treatment for chronic pain.

medications that use this metabolic pathway in the liver. In other words, consuming very large quantities of dandelion could allow toxic levels of the above medications to build up in the body, but a single cup of tea is considered safe for most people.

So often we accomplish a goal in life only to move right on to another one. Make a conscious resolution to celebrate the accomplishments of your climb during your tea ceremony. What challenges did you overcome? In what way did your skills improve today? How does this climb reflect your personal growth as a human? Decide to revel in the moment of *this* climb on *this* day before setting your sights on the next summit.

In Closing

As a midwesterner, my climbing experience has been limited to indoor climbing walls, an ice silo, and a few pitches on natural rock. Yet, of all the adventures I have been fortunate to have, I find that there is nothing quite like the rush and exhilaration of climbing.

On a recent outing with local climbing legends Don and Dianna Briggs to Backbone State Park in northeast Iowa, my husband Joe and I were moved by the couple's fabulous skill and their passion for sharing it with others. Don (who goes simply by "Briggs") is a retired university wrestling coach and climbing instructor, and is the creator of the infamous Iowa ice silo. Quoted in numerous publications, these words in a February 27, 2015, *Cedar Rapids Gazette* article seem to capture his approach to climbing and maybe even life: "Most importantly, don't give up. If you make it to the top, your arms screaming in pain, drink in the view. It's an accomplishment to relish."

On the subject of mindfulness and climbing, Dianna commented to me, "Any time I'm doing something outside, I get a sense of renewal. When we're rock climbing or ice climbing, we're focused on the challenge ahead of us and the good friends we're with. We truly feel a sense of gratitude."

As challenging as climbing is for me, I find that utilizing the elements of forest bathing helps to propel me upward when I think there's nothing left inside. Between the teachings of my mentors and the guidance of the more-than-human world, perhaps one day I will realize my lofty pipe dream of climbing (just a few hundred feet!) on El Capitan at Yosemite.

Facing page: Lessons from Briggs

CROSS-COUNTRY SKIING

I was about fourteen years old when I borrowed a pair of my parents' cross-country skis and set out for the snowy cemetery near our house. Although the boots were two sizes too big, I loved the feeling of gliding through snow. I remember imagining living in the Arctic using skis for transportation—what fun would that be? I fell into a soothing, harmonious cadence as I learned to coordinate skis and poles. Making first tracks through the immaculate fresh snow, I discovered, was exhilarating. I reveled in that special silence that only exists when snow muffles and blankets the world, and I was enthralled by the glistening glory of millions upon millions of minuscule, sparkling snowflakes. The slap of cold on my cheeks felt invigorating as the rest of my body warmed up. I loved this novel adventure.

Years later, as a way to embrace winter and avoid my annual tendency toward seasonal affective disorder, I decided to buy a pair of my own cross-country skis. Finding winter outdoor adventure has proven to be my salvation, whether it is in the form of cross-country skiing, snowshoeing, or fat biking. The experience of peacefully moving through the woods in and among a backdrop of fresh snow is simply breathtaking, invigorating, and lifesaving for me.

Although this chapter focuses on the sport of cross-country skiing, many of the forest bathing invitations—and certainly the plant medicine—can be applied to many other winter activities.

History and Stewardship

Cross-country skiing was the first form of skiing and was initially used as a form of transportation through snow. According to the Olympic Games website (www.olympic.org), the first skis were devised in Norway, where the Norwegian word *skid* refers to a split piece of wood. Skiing as a sport first occurred in the mid-1800s, with the first recorded race taking place in 1842 in Norway. Men's cross-country skiing was added to the Olympics in 1924, with the women's event added in 1952.

Today, cross-country skiing is often combined with other forms of skiing, as well as snowboarding, in organizations that govern and regulate the sports.

Since 1905 the US Ski and Snowboard Association (www.usskiandsnowboard.org) has supported skiers—and now snowboarders—within the United States, "committed to the progression of its sports, athlete success and the value of team." In October 2017 it released a sustainability statement recognizing the impact of climate change on the practice of its winter sports. Within this statement, the organization pledges that "we will tackle climate change by reducing our environmental footprint and promoting environmental responsibility."

On a global level, the International Ski Federation (FIS; www.fis-ski.com) is the largest governing body for international winter sports, including alpine skiing, cross-country skiing, ski jumping, and snowboarding, among others. Now based in Switzerland, FIS was founded in Norway in 1910 and is currently responsible for setting international rules of competition. Environmentalism and climate change have become issues of concern for this international coalition, which has sought to achieve ISO (International Organization for Standardization) sustainability certification for their upcoming world competitions.

Matters related to climate change, environmental conservation, and sustainability have not always been a top consideration or priority within the skiing community. With the past several years showing the hottest temperatures in recorded history, the Northern Hemisphere has lost a million square miles of spring snowpack since the year 1970, an area that is three times the size of Texas. According to climatologist Daniel Scott from the University of Waterloo in Ontario, within thirty years the western United States is estimated to lose 25 to 100 percent of its snowpack if greenhouse gas emissions are not markedly reduced. This translates to winters with a complete lack of snow in areas such as Park City, Utah, and "relegating skiing to the top quarter of Ajax Mountain in Aspen [Colorado]," according to a February 7, 2014, article in the *New York Times*. The sobering downstream implications of this, of course, are a lack of drinking water, drought, and forest fires, among many, many other disastrous effects well beyond the ability to ski.

In response to climate change, professional snowboarder Jeremy Jones founded the organization Protect Our Winters (www.protectourwinters.org) in 2007. As explained on its website, "Jones found that more and more resorts he'd always counted on for good riding were closed due to lack of snow. Something was clearly going on, and he felt the need to act. But he couldn't find any organizations focused on mobilizing the snow sports community on climate—there was a gap between the impacts that climate change was already having on our mountains, and any organized action being taken to address it." Today, Protect Our Winters has grown into "a network of over 130,000 supporters—a social movement on climate, designed to activate a

I spoke with the Reverend Scott Duffus, a multisport endurance athlete, a pastor, and an outdoor enthusiast. In addition to being an avid ultrarunner, kayaker, and mountain biker, Scott has raced in numerous cross-country ski and snowshoe races, including the famous American Birkebeiner, North America's largest cross-country ski race, which he has raced at least seven times. He has competed in cross-country ski races all over the United States, often completing six to seven races in a season.

I asked Scott about his penchant for outdoor adventure. He answered, "I have all of the gadgets of a modern endurance athlete. I measure heart rate and power. I upload my workouts to Garmin Connect, TrainingPeaks, and Strava. I have a high-end treadmill, and I am in the market for a smart trainer for my bicycle. But the truth is I very much prefer the outdoors. For me it is not really just about the exercise, it is about the experience. In some ways I have not figured out why being outdoors is such a big factor for me because I measure and keep track of so many things. But even if it is below zero or windy or rainy or muddy, I would rather be outdoors.

"I have been doing things outdoors all of my life," Scott went on to say, when pressed about the influence of nature and the concept of forest bathing. "When I smell black spruce, it is like a comforting truth that connects back to my youth and all of the time I spent in northern Minnesota. I run through a grove of aspen trees and it is almost as though I can feel their roots connected in the common organism that they are. Even the nettles that inhabit some of my favorite local trails remind me of all of the time I spent in the Minnesota river bottoms as a kid. Until relatively recently, I had never heard of forest bathing, but I think I have been experiencing elements of it all of my life. It is a matter of connection for me."

I also asked Scott how time spent in nature seemed to affect his health and well-being, both physically and mentally. He replied, "I am diverse as an athlete. I ride road, gravel, mountain, and fat bikes. I ski and snowshoe competitively. I canoe and kayak competitively, and my base for all of this is running. I am in pretty good physical shape for a sixty-one-year-old male, and that is important to me. But in a lot of ways it is how the hour or two of physical training I commit to on most days changes my mindset, and in the end that is probably the bigger benefit for me.

"Cross-country skiing is a very technique-dependent sport," he continued. "I have spent hours in clinics and with coaches working on the intricacies of all of that, but in the end, it gets to a place where you do not think about it at all. Your body is invested in a physical mantra that requires a high heart rate to support. In a way, your focus narrows. I think I ski right past plenty that I would not miss during a leisurely walk, but you also inhabit a very connected place in space and time [when you ski]."

passionate community and create the political will for meaningful action by state and federal policymakers."

Perhaps through the voices of environmental activists and celebrity athletes and the recent collaboration between skiing organizations and groups such as Protect Our Winters, policy makers will heed these warnings. In the meantime, we can all work to do our part to turn the ship of climate change around.

Mindfulness in Cross-Country Skiing

I find that there is just enough rhythm in the gliding motion of traditional cross-country skiing to lull my senses into a mindful state. Couple that with the strikingly silent stillness of the woods in winter, and one can get lost (figuratively if not literally) for hours. The fact that cross-country skiing transpires at a slower pace (at least for me!) than some other forms of outdoor adventure makes it highly amenable to the application of forest bathing.

FOREST BATHING/SHINRIN-YOKU AND CROSS-COUNTRY SKIING

INVITATIONS BEFORE CROSS-COUNTRY SKIING
Pleasures of Presence

New-fallen snow can be breathtaking to behold. Why not fully take it in, through all of your senses, before setting out to ski? Prior to doing so, consider adding an extra layer of clothing. Cross-country skiing warms the body quickly; forest bathing does not!

There are options for preparing to forest bathe in snow. You may choose to sit directly on the ground, on a chair, or on any other suitable object. You may choose to remain standing. I recommend performing the "Pleasures of Presence" invitation prior to donning your skis.

Invitation: Once you are situated, begin by closing your eyes and taking some slow, deep breaths. Take a moment, as you do this, to contemplate your physical location and the ancestral history of the area, and to acknowledge the humans who inhabited this place decades and centuries before you. Take a moment, also, to acknowledge the trees, plants, animals, birds, insects, and other beings in the more-than-human world that call this place their home. Take a moment, finally, to acknowledge Mother Earth and all of the components that must come together to provide snow for your enjoyment. Imagine a world devoid of snow and consider offering up some gratitude for our planet and the forces of nature that tend it.

Open your eyes for a moment, and take your gloved hands and scoop up a handful of snow. Closing your eyes again, notice the way the snow feels as you hold it in your hands. Can you feel the cold temperature of the snow through your gloves? With gloves on, can you appreciate the texture of the snow? Is it dry and somewhat crunchy, or does it feel wet and slushy? With eyes closed, can you tell if you could pack this snow into a snowball, or will it simply crumble apart? Notice how heavy the snow is. Can you pass it between your two hands and appreciate its weight? What does it feel like if you let some of the snow fall between your fingers?

Next, gather some more snow if you need to and bring it up to your face. What does the snow smell like? If you touch the snow to your nose or cheek, what does that feel like? Does it melt when it touches your skin? Does it fall right off? How does touching it to your face compare with holding it in your gloved hands? Next, bring the snow to your lips and touch it to your lips. What does that feel like, with respect to temperature, texture, weight? Stick out your tongue, then, and touch the snow to your tongue. Notice not only the taste of snow but also the way it feels to touch the snow to your tongue. Does this bring back any memories? What else do you notice?.

Now, bring a handful of snow up to your ear. Holding it motionless next to your ear, does your handful of snow make a sound? If you squeeze the snow with your hand, what does that sound like? Does it make a creaking sound or more like a squishing sound? What does it sound like if you let the snow fall to the ground from your hands? What else do you notice about the *sounds* of snow?

Finally, bring a handful of snow toward your lap or to the level of your abdomen if you are standing. Hold it in your hands with eyes closed. If you grew up in a warm climate without snow, this may resonate with you. If not, imagine that you did just arrive here from a tropical climate and have never, in your life, experienced snow. Prepare to open your eyes and *see* snow, as if for the very first time. Give yourself a count of three, and then open your eyes. What is it like to see snow for the very first time?

When you feel that you have completed the Pleasures of Presence, take a moment to reflect upon the sights, sounds, tastes, smells, and tactile characteristics of snow along with any observations or revelations that may have occurred. Take a moment to share with a partner, to journal, or to take a few notes about your experience.

What's in Motion?

Especially effective in winter, when it seems that signs of life are limited, "What's in Motion?" never disappoints.

Invitation: Before setting out, take a moment to notice what is in motion. Set a timer for ten minutes or so and take a short, slow walk taking in what, visibly, is in motion. It may be necessary to position yourself so that you can examine a barren tree, shrub, or grasses up close and take some time to wait and really seek signs of motion. If your attention is pulled away, gently remind yourself to return to the task of finding visible signs of movement. At the completion of your invitation, ask yourself what you noticed. Prior to setting out on skis, journal or jot some notes about your experience with "What's in Motion?"

Snow Angels

When was the last time you made a snow angel? You are hereby invited to return to your childhood for a moment.

Invitation: Lie on the ground in the snow facing upward. Starting with your hands straight down by your sides, simultaneously arc your arms overhead while opening and closing your straightened legs. Return your

Snow angels at Briggs Woods Lake, Hamilton County, Iowa

arms and legs to the midline and repeat, several times. Press your head into the snow to create an imprint and then stop all movement, in any position that feels right with your arms and legs. Lie in complete stillness in the snow and close your eyes for a moment. Notice the sensation of your body where it is in contact with the snow. Surrender all of your weight to the snow, and appreciate what that feels like. Notice the temperature of the snow and the temperature of the air. Is there any snow falling? What does it feel like to have snow falling on your face? Stick out your tongue, if you wish, and see if you can catch a snowflake.

When you are ready, go ahead and open your eyes and spend a moment simply gazing upward. Take in the clouds, tree branches, any birds overhead, or the sight of falling snow, for as long as you wish. When you are finished, step carefully away so as to preserve your angel and then survey your work. What is it like to make angels in the snow?

INVITATIONS DURING CROSS-COUNTRY SKIING
Pleasures of Presence

During the time that you are skiing, whether at the beginning, middle, or end of your outing, be sure to practice the Pleasures of Presence in some way. This practice will heighten your overall awareness and bring mindfulness to your adventure, and can help pass the time and keep your mind off any physical miseries if you are racing. You may choose to focus on a particular sense for a set period of time, or you may wish to follow the invitation as described below.

Invitation: As you are skiing, notice the quality of your breath. Is it deep and rhythmic or short, shallow, and choppy? Concentrate, first, on evening out your breath so that you are completely exhaling before starting to inhale. You may also wish to count along with your breathing so that the length of exhalation is equal to, if not longer than, the length of inhalation. Commit to fully expanding your lungs with each inhalation and notice a rhythm beginning to develop.

Continuing with slow, rhythmic breaths, begin to notice the quality of the air that is entering your nose. What is the temperature? Is it colder than your body temperature, and if so, how cold is it? Does it burn your nasal passages, it is so cold, or is it more tolerably cool? What is the water content of the air? Is it moist and humid or dry? Is there wind or is the air around you fairly still? What does the air smell like? Can you smell soil, plants, or animals? Can you smell the snow? What does snow actually smell like? Do you notice other scents, such as the smell of your clothing? Are there other ambient fragrances? Imagine that you could hold all these scents together and simultaneously bring them into your body as you breathe. Appreciate that you are breathing in the same air that the nearby plants, animals, and other beings are breathing, even if much of winter wildlife appears to be dormant. It is all still very much alive.

Next, as you glide through the snow, start noticing the sounds in your midst. Begin by paying attention to the sound of your breathing, once more, and by noticing any other internal sounds within your body. Can you hear your heart beating or your stomach growling? What other internal sounds can you pick up if you listen carefully? Next, notice the sound your clothing makes as you move through the snow. Allow yourself to fall into the rhythm of your clothing as you move within it. Allow, then, the rhythm of your clothing to give way to the rhythm of your skis moving through the snow. What kind of sound do your skis make? Permit yourself to become immersed in the sound of your skis gliding through the snow for as long as you like. Is the sound even from side to side? If not, or if the sound is more choppy than smooth, what can you do to improve the rhythm and quality

of the sound of your skiing? What does this do for your efficiency of motion? What other sounds do you hear as you ski? Can you hear the movement of trees or plants? Is there running water nearby? Can you hear the dripping of melting ice? What signs of bird or animal life do you hear? What other sounds do you notice while skiing?

Decide, next, that you will focus on the visual aspects of skiing. Notice colors, patterns, brightness, and any other contrasts you can find. Look up, look down, look right, look left. Follow movement and follow your curiosity.

Take a set period of time to focus solely on your sense of smell. Resist the temptation to be distracted by other sensory input and concentrate on taking in the scents of your surroundings. Notice if the scents are consistent during your outing or if they change as you go.

Finally, pay attention to physical sensations. You may choose to start at the top of your head and move down, noticing a variety of physical findings. For example, you may choose to focus on the sensation of your clothing touching your various body parts, from the top of your head all the way down to the soles of your feet. You may explore body temperature, muscle tension, and joint and muscle fatigue in the same way, from top to bottom. Attempt to notice these sensations, without judgment, as you scan up or down the body.

What transpired during your Pleasures of Presence on skis? Did time pass more quickly or efficiently? Did any questions arise? Were any memories triggered? What else did you notice?

What's in Motion?

Not only is your body propelling through the woods, but there is movement surrounding you even on the most tranquil of days. In winter, it is possible to see much deeper into a deciduous forest, thanks to the lack of leaves and underbrush.

Invitation: While you ski, set the intention to watch for signs of motion for a certain period of time or for a specific distance. As it is practical, take turns setting your gaze at different distances: far, near, up, down. Soften your gaze, or even squint your eyes, to notice signs of motion. What do you notice?

Forest Shadows

The angle of the sun in winter makes for long, dramatic shadows in early morning and late afternoon. These shadows can make it feel almost as if you were suspended in time and space, and can seem to beckon you deeper into the forest.

Invitation: As you ski, concentrate your attention on looking *only* at shadows, as opposed to noticing the object that is creating the shadow. Appreciate the different perspective that is afforded by shadow seeking. What is the largest shadow you can find? How small is the smallest shadow you can see? Do you notice moving shadows or only static shadows? What does your own shadow look like? What discoveries do you make about shadows?

Icicle Inspirations

Have you ever watched water dripping off an icicle? They drip so slowly and freeze as they drip, so that one minute's drip becomes the next minute's icicle. Observing this process while actively moving could be a challenge but, when conditions are right, simply searching for icicles while skiing can be spellbinding.

Invitation: Seek high and seek low. Can you hear the rhythmic trickling of water that forms icicles? Where do you see icicles as you ski? Are there tiny, miniature versions of icicles that you might never have thought to notice before? Break an icicle off and examine it. What do

you notice about the way it looks? How does it feel in your hands? Have you ever sucked on an icicle before? How might an icicle be a metaphor for life?

Is Everything Black and White?

There is something stunning about the contrast of white snow on bare black trees in winter. In fact, simply taking in the beauty of new-fallen snow and the divine way that every minute surface is evenly covered is a forest bathing invitation in and of itself. I have spent entire cross-country skiing outings doing nothing but taking it in.

Invitation: If at some point your mind requires variety, look high and low for the possibility of any other color. A red cardinal, a blue jay, a green leaf somehow clinging to life, or even an orange reflector or a blue mailbox can seem like the rewards of a scavenger hunt. What is it like to find glimpses of color in a sea of black and white?

Signs of Life

Whether it is fall, winter, or spring, I enjoy searching for signs of life. In the "dead" of winter, signs of life are trickier to spot . . . but they are there!

Invitation: As you ski, imagine that you are a wildlife tracker, setting out to find signs of life. Look for animal tracks. Can you name the animal(s) that created them? Where do you suppose they were going? Discover animal droppings. Who made those? Are there any signs (even dormant) of insects? Do you see birds flying? Are there feathers or nests, or other signs that birds have been here? What about plant life? Is there any green peeking out of the brown? Are there buds forming on trees or shrubs if you look closely? Do you see any moss at all? How about mushrooms or fungi? Are there signs of *human* life? What are you noticing about signs of life in winter? How does it make you feel?

Every Breath You Take

In reading my friend and fellow forest therapy guide Melanie Choukas-Bradley's book *The Joy of Forest Bathing*, I was struck by her phrase "the inward and outer worlds connected by your own steamy breath" when forest bathing in winter. I underlined it and read it over and over. Contemplating this profound notion gave rise to an invitation I have since explored during cold weather.

Invitation: As you ski, pay attention to "your own steamy breath" and simply sense the connection between your inner and outer worlds. One could go on for miles, simply pondering that relationship.

If that does not offer enough food for thought, consider, as you sense the moisture, the warmth, and the visible foggy swirl of your breath, the root of the word *respiration*. The Latin *spir* means "to breathe." What other words can you think of that have the same root word (*respiration*, to breathe in and out, again and again; *expire*, to breathe one's last breath; *perspire*, to "breathe" through one's pores; *transpire*, *conspire*, *aspire* . . .)?

Did you know that the word *spirit* comes from the same root? What, if anything, does that mean to you? Notice any thoughts that are provoked when contemplating these words and associations. Continue to observe the connection of your inner and outer worlds through your own steamy breath.

INVITATIONS AFTER CROSS-COUNTRY SKIING
Sit Spot
There is nothing quite like a snowy Sit Spot. If the opportunity arises, find a place to sit that is near water, whether it is frozen, semi-frozen, or flowing. Use a mat or a chair, if you can, to keep warm. Or, if your clothing is adequately insulated, make yourself comfortable right down in the snow. Once you have found the perfect sit spot, set a timer for at least twenty minutes. Enjoy the opportunity to do absolutely nothing but sit and absorb the winter wonderland. Complete the invitation by journaling when your time is up. What did you notice during Sit Spot? What was it like to forest bathe as a cross-country skier? How do you feel physically and mentally?

Snow Sculpture
After Sit Spot, take a moment to reflect on your forest bathing ski outing. Was there a moment that was especially memorable in some way? Did something make you laugh? Were you reminded of a childhood experience or a special person? Did something catch your eye simply because of its sheer beauty? Take the time to create a snow sculpture that reflects your special moment, in whatever way you choose to memorialize it. There is no judge, no critique, of your art. You may

even smash it when you are done if you prefer it to remain private, or you may choose to leave your sculpture for others to enjoy. If you are with other people, feel free to share your sculptures and your memorable moments with each other.

TEA CEREMONY: PINE

In winter, the options for tea ceremony can be sparse. If there are pine trees nearby, though, you are set. Pine needle tea is an aromatic option that is packed with nutrition.

There is a variety of pine species in the United States and other parts of the world. It is important to have a general understanding of evergreen trees, however, because not all of them are edible. Yews, for instance, are highly poisonous if one consumes the needles, bark, or seeds, due to their deadly taxine alkaloids. See the Herbal Insight sidebar for some quick tips for identifying evergreens.

Herbal Insight: Pine, Spruce, Fir, Yew . . . Which Is It?

Pine trees can be distinguished from other evergreen trees by comparing needles. Pines tend to have the longest needles, ranging from around one to ten inches in length, which are arranged in bundles, or fascicles. The specific species of pine can be determined by first counting the number of needles per fascicle. Eastern white pine typically has five needles per fascicle, red pine has two needles, Scotch pine has two, ponderosa pine has three, and so on. Additional characteristics, such as the length of the needle and the appearance of the bark and pinecone, can then confirm the species.

In contrast to pine trees, spruce (*Picea* spp.) and fir (*Abies* spp.) trees have needles that grow individually from the branch (in other words, not in fascicles). Both are members of the Pinaceae family along with pines. Fir needles are flat, blunt-tipped, and grow upward, and there is a noticeable lack of needles on the underside of a fir branch. Conversely, spruce trees' needles have four sides and can be rolled between your fingers. They also grow in a whorled pattern around the entire branch.

Like pine, fir trees have edible parts with medicinal properties. Also, like pine, fir is high in vitamin C and has been used to prevent and treat scurvy. The resin has antiseptic and analgesic (pain-killing) properties and can be topically applied to wounds, sores, burns, and bruises. Fir needles can be used to make tea, and the inner bark can be cooked and eaten.

Yews (*Taxus* spp.) are an entirely different story. These trees and shrubs belong to the Taxaceae family. Although yew berries are edible, the entire rest of the tree is poisonous, including the seeds within the berries. In contrast to yews, hemlock trees (*Tsuga* spp., members of the Pinaceae family) have slightly shorter, flat needles but have white stripes similar to fir needles. Yew needles are completely green and lack any white stripes whatsoever. Note that

Spruce sprig

Juniper bush with berries

the poisonous hemlock (*Conium maculatum*, of the parsley, or Apiaceae, family) is an herbaceous plant and not an evergreen at all. The *Tsuga* hemlock species of the pine family are not at all poisonous. A poultice made from the inner bark of evergreen hemlock can act as an astringent and a styptic, useful for stopping bleeding and speeding the healing of wounds.

Finally are the junipers and new-world cedars, which both belong to the Cupressaceae family. While eastern red cedars are, in actuality, junipers (Latin name *Juniperus virginiana*), Mediterranean "true cedars" (*Cedrus* spp.) are not native to the United States and actually belong to the Pineceae, or pine, family.

New-world cedars (again, of the Cupressaceae family) are native to North America and include the western red cedar, Atlantic white cedar, northern white cedar (or arborvitae), dawn redwood, and giant sequoia. We owe this mass confusion to the early North American settlers who apparently had little understanding of taxonomy! This all makes me chuckle, as my home town of Cedar Falls is named for the eastern red cedar that lines the Cedar River in Iowa. Since the eastern red cedar is really a juniper, I guess it should have been named the *Juniper* River and *Juniper* Falls!

As for ingesting junipers and cedars, they are all edible. Juniper tea made from needles and berries has both diuretic (urine-stimulating) and antimicrobial (germ-fighting) qualities. Juniper is also often used by herbalists for various kidney remedies. The juniper berry is not a true berry at all, but is actually the female seed cone. Used as a spice in some countries, the juniper berry has been used since the seventeenth century to make gin.

So, barring the poisonous yew, it is fun to know that most evergreens are not only edible but hold an abundance of medicinal properties. Just be *sure* to know your yews!

Fir branch

The branch and berries of a yew tree

The Science of Nature: Stress Relief—Happy Parents, Healthy Kids

For those of us who spend a great deal of time outdoors, it seems obvious that nature acts as a potent stress reliever. But for low-income parents in urban areas, could a prescription to spend time in a park reduce stress, serve as an antidote to loneliness, and translate to better health outcomes?

The "Stay Healthy in Nature Everyday (SHINE)" study published in 2018 by Dr. Nooshin Razani and her colleagues at UCSF Benioff Children's Hospital Oakland, sought to address the fact that stress in low-income parents and their children has been recognized as a contributing factor to health outcome disparities. Social isolation is known to compound these issues. As stated in their report, "With more than 46.7 million people living in poverty in the United States, innovative, community-based means of dealing with stress are needed in this population."

This prospective randomized study of seventy-eight parents was conducted to determine whether a prescription to spend time in a park would improve stress and other behavioral and health outcomes. The prescription included a recommendation by a physician, a map of local parks, a journal, and a pedometer. The researchers offered group park outings for one arm of the study and the prescription alone, with no group visits, in the other arm. Outcomes were measured by question-naires for stress and loneliness (the forty-point Perceived Stress Scale and the Modified UCLA Loneliness Scale, respectively), as well as salivary cortisol levels as a measure of physiologic stress.

The study found a decrease in parental stress, both overall and as a function of the number of park visits per week. Interestingly, the park prescription *without* group park visits resulted in more weekly park visits than did the arm that included group visits. In other words, sim-ply recommending that parents and their kids head out to a park was more effective than inviting them to a group park outing.

The authors acknowledge that larger trials are needed to under-stand these relationships further, but it seems safe to say that some-thing as simple as a doctor recommending time spent in nature can have mental and physical health benefits that transcend generations.

Pine trees belong to the genus *Pinus*, of the family Pinaceae. There are over a hundred species worldwide, with some common native North American species being the eastern white pine, the western white pine, and red, sugar, lodgepole, and ponderosa pines. Nonnative pines are also now commonly found in the United States, such as the Scots (or Scotch) pine.

To make a pine needle tea, begin by wild-tending some bunches of needles and completely fill your tea vessel with them. Add nearly boiling water and steep for about five minutes. You will notice the pine needles losing some of their green color as they steep.

Before tasting the tea, cup your hand over the top and savor the aroma. Does it evoke any memories or emotions? When you taste your tea, know that you are ingesting a healthy dose of vitamin C. In fact, historically, pine needle tea was used for prevention and treatment of scurvy. It might not even surprise you to know that pine needle tea has been used over time to treat respiratory illnesses as a decongestant and expectorant, and that pine has been found to be an effective antiseptic (think Pine-Sol).

What thoughts, ideas, or revelations arise from your experience with pine needle tea?

In Closing

When I reflect upon my experiences with cross-country skiing, snow-shoeing, and other winter adventures, my first thought is to recognize just how much these activities have saved me from the doldrums of winter. I don't need studies to personally know that time spent outdoors is critical to my mental and physical health, especially in the winter.

A close-second thought is a recognition that winters are so, so critical to our global ecosystem. Whether or not I complain about cold weather and dream of escaping winter, the thought of a world without snow, ice, and glaciers is beyond depressing. No amount of seasonal affective disorder can begin to rival that level of planetary despair.

My family and I do what we can to reduce our carbon footprint, making improvements each and every year. We support and contribute to organizations that reflect our environmental values and vote in favor of leaders who "get it." We also get outside every chance we can to enjoy and cherish the wild places. It is a reciprocal relationship that we recognize as crucial: As we take care of nature, nature takes care of us.

TRAIL RUNNING

I hated running as a kid. I still have traumatic memories of track-and-field day, trying to sprint or (God forbid) run hurdles on a track. I was never fast. I never believed running was something I could ever do. Not long after my husband was diagnosed with Stage IV lung cancer, though, running became something of a metaphorical answer to life's challenges. After Dave passed away, I ran my first half marathon. Shortly after that, I discovered running on dirt. It was a novel, beautiful, and liberating concept to me. I created a trail running mantra that gave gratitude to my health, my children, and to Dave that I would repeat over and over when running became difficult. To this day, when I'm running, the mantra often just auto-plays. It's longer now, as a whole new chapter of life has begun, with many more names to add.

It is estimated that 146.1 million Americans, or 49 percent of the US population, participated in an outdoor activity at least once in 2017, according to the 2018 annual Outdoor Participation Report published by the Outdoor Foundation (www.outdoorfoundation.org). Running, including jogging and trail running, was the most popular activity among Americans when measured by both number of participants and number of total annual outings.

There are a number of reasons why people across the globe are turning to trail running, which, essentially, involves running and hiking over dirt trails as opposed to running on pavement or tracks. The larger ascents and descents afforded by often-mountainous terrain make trail running an adventurous sport. Trail runners also cite less trauma to muscles and joints, as well as the interaction with nature, as benefits to trail running. In fact, a survey of my local chapter of Trail Sisters, a national women's trail running organization, www.trailsisters.net, showed the following reasons they prefer trail running over running on pavement (respondents could choose as many options as they felt applied): 91 percent reported "being out in nature does it for me," 55 percent cited less impact on joints and muscles, 23 percent noted their desire to be involved in races that are environmentally friendly, and 27 percent cited "other" reasons. Some of the "other" comments included: "I love feeling like a wild animal running through the woods!" "The community of other trail runners is amazing." "No noise, no cars, no people. Escapism." "It's a bit more challenging. I enjoy jumping over logs, going over bridges, or slopping through water crossings. Makes you feel like a kid!"

I also asked the Trail Sisters if they ever used sensory elements from nature to help them pass the time. Here are some of their responses: "Sometimes in a race I set goals on the trail to pass the time, like 'just run in the sun to the shade and then walk and rest a bit.'" "I like identifying plants and looking for small insects on the trail. Finding snails are the best! Imagining where the animals live. Thinking of who was here before me." "I love listening for different birds. During a recent adventure Tri, I heard an eagle or hawk calling and it immediately helped me pick up my pace. I felt like 'she' was cheering me on." "I'm constantly looking and listening for wildlife. I love observing animals in their natural habitat." "I like looking at the play of light on objects." It sounds as if the Trail Sisters have forest bathing figured out!

Echoing the sentiments of the Trail Sisters, my friend, avid runner, personal trainer, and nature lover Rebecca Schultze wrote this:

Moving over rocks, dirt, roots, and fallen trees brings me peace, freedom, joy, awe, and wonder. You can't zone out and go through the motions; it requires presence and an awareness of your body and your surroundings. And yet there's an ease to running over natural terrain that I've never experienced on a treadmill or on pavement. Somehow focusing on movement over unpredictable terrain frees my mind from stress-inducing thoughts and opens my heart to wonder.

I grew up on a national wildlife refuge, free from the constraints of city streets and sidewalks, so perhaps that's why, even as an adult, time in nature fuels my soul and brings me back to my truest self. When I find myself agitated, restless, anxious, or trending toward indifference to the things and people I love, the antidote is sun on my face, wind in my hair, and dirt on my skin. Every run brings me joy on some level, but it's the runs through a more natural world that throw large doses of awe and amazement into the mix. Each run outside of civilization brings a heightened sense of knowing that things can go wrong, that Mother Nature is fickle and unpredictable, that uncertainty makes me feel vulnerable and alive in a way that manicured lawns, paved roads, and timed stoplights can't rival.

Disconnecting from civilization allows me to reconnect to my instincts. The rustling of grass on a calm day instantly perks me up; a deep rumble from the sky sends adrenaline through my veins. And I believe this is good for me, that it's healthy to light up my survival instincts now and then so that they'll be primed for circumstances in which I truly do need them.

History and Trail Stewardship

Trail running races can include distances from 5 kilometers (3.1 miles) all the way to various forms of "ultra" races, which are defined as anything longer than a marathon distance, or 26.2 miles. Common ultra distances include 50 kilometers (31.1 miles), 100 kilometers (62.1 miles), 50 miles, and 100 miles. There are also timed races, such as 24-hour races, as well as multiday races of 1,000 miles or greater.

Trail runners are often able to run close to home on hiking trails at local parks. Many runners also travel specifically to explore new trails. At the time of this writing, the Trail Run Project (www.trailrunproject.com) boasts having maps of over 150,000 miles in over 40,000 trails all over the world. Trail runners are able to add to the website and app to share trail information with fellow runners.

The American Trail Running Association (ATRA) was established in 1996 with the mission of representing and promoting safe, fun, and sustainable mountain, ultra, and trail running. Its website, www.trailrunner.com, contains the largest trail race event calendar online, and members receive the *Trail Times* newsletter with information on upcoming events, articles, and news related to the sport.

On a global level, the International Trail Running Association (ITRA; https://itra.run) and the International Association of Ultrarunners (IAU; www.iau-ultramarathon.org) are organizations that govern and host international trail running races.

As with any sport that uses trails through public lands, trail stewardship is an imperative concern for trail runners. ATRA declared the theme for 2018 to be "Trail Stewardship: Leaving a Lasting Legacy." As stated on its website by executive director Nancy Hobbs, "It is imperative that we all work together to take care of the trails we so cherish, or there won't be opportunities for future generations to enjoy

our growing sport." Over the course of the year, ATRA featured clubs, individuals, and events that helped maintain the trails through active volunteerism. Additionally, it made a point to highlight events that required race participants to do volunteer work in order to secure a race entry. "Sharing these events and their stories provides a model for others to follow suit and create their own programs," Hobbs said.

The world's first ultra-endurance race was the Western States 100-Mile Endurance Run, held annually in California. Started in 1974, this race challenges runners to climb more than 18,000 feet and descend nearly 23,000 feet along the historic Western States Trail, making it one of the greatest tests of endurance in the world. Guiding the way for other events to follow suit, the Western States created a foundation, known as the Western States Endurance Run Foundation (WSERF; www.wser.org), whose goal is to "conserve and contribute

The Science of Nature: Stress Detox

Did you know that there is a growing body of evidence demonstrating the mental health benefits of time spent in nature? One of these studies looked at 498 healthy volunteers before and after participating in forest bathing. Participants completed two surveys that are commonly used to assess symptoms of depression and anxiety (the Multiple Mood Scale–Short Form and the State-Trait Anxiety Inventory A-State Scale). The same participants took both surveys twice in one day while forest bathing, and twice in one day on a "control" day.

Results showed statistically significant improvement in all parameters of mental health, such as stress level, hostility, depression, and feeling of liveliness during and after forest bathing as compared to the control day. It was even found that the greater the magnitude of stress, the greater the benefit of forest bathing for these participants (Morita et al. 2007).

So, the next time life has you feeling anxious or depressed, remember to explore the mind-altering effects of some forest therapy. You can't overdose on this one!

to the management of the trail and surrounding environs in a manner that balances local, state and federal agency priorities, respects historic conditions and promotes responsible public use and safety," according to its website. The foundation works in collaboration with the US Forest Service, California Department of Parks and Recreation, Western States Trail Foundation, and the Placer County Water Agency to ensure that various interests are maintained throughout this process.

Mindfulness in Trail Running

Mindfulness, or (most simply) paying attention to nothing but the present moment, is something that most trail runners agree is not only critically important for safety, but is also something that gets them through long runs and keeps them returning to their sport. Safety factors into mindful trail running in a number of ways: Keeping an eye on the trail prevents injury by avoiding roots and slippery or loose rocks, and being mindful of surroundings avoids collisions with animals and other humans. Returning one's thoughts to the present moment prevents the mind from dwelling on the day's troubles and from focusing on physical discomfort. And when trail runners are interviewed, it seems that it is this ability to be lost in the moment that makes them regularly train and seek new trail running challenges.

FOREST BATHING/SHINRIN-YOKU AND TRAIL RUNNING

INVITATIONS BEFORE RUNNING
Pleasures of Presence

Before setting out on a trail run, taking a moment to separate from the stressors of the day can set the tone for an experience that is both physically and mentally healing. The "Pleasures of Presence" invitation is an effective way to leave those stressors behind.

Invitation: Begin by looking around and locating a stone that you find yourself drawn to. This stone should be small enough that it can fit in one hand. Go ahead and pick it up. If your trail has no stones, any natural object will also work. Feel free to stand or sit for this invitation.

Once you are comfortably positioned, begin by closing your eyes. Hold the stone either in your lap or in your hand, relaxed at your side.

I had the opportunity to interview trail running legend Scott Jurek in preparation for this book. To summarize his numerous accomplishments, I turned to his website, www.scottjurek.com, where they were distilled down to the highlights: "He has claimed victories in nearly all of ultrarunning's elite trail and road events including the historic 153-mile Spartathlon, the Hardrock 100, the Badwater 135-Mile Ultramarathon, and—his signature race—the Western States 100-Mile Endurance Run, which he won a record seven straight times. Scott has also taken the running world by storm with his 2015 Appalachian Trail speed record, averaging nearly 50 miles a day over 46 days—and the United States all-surface record in the 24-Hour Run with 165.7 miles: 6.5 marathons in one day."

I asked Scott if he could explain ways in which mindfulness factors into his running. His response: "Having that sense of tactile sensation with my feet, specifically, is really key. Other aspects, like vision and sight, and paying attention to body movements, is something that I feel like if I didn't do that, I wouldn't be as good a runner. So, from a performance standpoint, I've really encouraged myself to pay attention to those details."

He went on to say, "There's still usually some time for me to stop and really take things in . . . Sometimes that might be a picturesque view, or something, but also just being immersed in the sounds. I feel like I've always been a bit more anti-headphone, when it comes to trail running, out of safety and also because I want to hear things around me. And so, the sounds, definitely, are something I've felt I've been in touch with.

"Then when I've done these really big challenges, where I've pushed my physical and mental abilities to the max, like the Appalachian Trail run, for instance, I feel like my senses were on this super-heightened aware state, because of the physical distress, the mental loads that I was putting on my body to do something over and over each day. I don't put myself in that situation a lot but when I have, the biggest thing I noticed is that my movements, my sense of smell, my sense of hearing, were really attuned in those moments. I think that by putting myself in that situation of where—I guess I'd have to say—it was like everything else had to let go, I could focus or let my body be in a primal survival state, where we used to have to pay attention to small details through our senses. So, I feel like, yeah, on one hand when I'm very comfortable on a training run, or pretty comfortable, and then on the other hand with the extreme example of something where I'm really stretching myself physically, that's where I've noticed that I've had this super-aware state, whether you want to call it the 'zone' or the 'flow state.' I've felt like the senses have opened up then. It's really quite magical."

I asked Scott, "In what way do you find nature to be healing?" He replied, "I think for me it's physically, mentally, spiritually—I feel like on all levels—it's healing, and sometimes I recognize more of those aspects than others. But to me, I feel like it's . . . I know it's good for me. I know something happens and I can't always explain it. Sometimes it's just happening and I feel like there's a reason I'm drawn to it." He continued, "So, for me . . . I feel like it's helped me out on so many levels. I can see it, too, in my two-year-old daughter, or even having a newborn for the past five months . . . we've brought them outside and even having them look at trees and stuff calms them down, versus being inside. So, it's one of those things where you're wondering at two in the morning what's going to get them to stop crying. It's funny: Both of our kids, we just brought 'em outside right away and they'd stop crying. So, I feel like it's healing on so many levels and I know—you're delving into the research so much more—but I know that for me, things are happening and it's beneficial, and there's got to be a reason that we're drawn to it. It sounds like you're helping answer some of that."

Start by taking some slow, deep breaths, bringing the air from your natural setting deep into your lungs.

Next, bring the stone up to chest level and hold it in both of your hands. Pass it gently between your two hands, noticing the weight of your stone. Is it heavy or lightweight? While passing it between your two hands, what else do you notice about the tactile sensations of your stone? Is it smooth or rough? Does it have sharp points, or has it been worn down to rounded edges? Can you imagine the forces throughout the millennia that transported and shaped this stone? Does your stone feel like it is made up of composites of minerals and smaller stones, or does it feel uniform in composition? Do you wonder how it was created? Does your stone have dirt or sand on it, or is it relatively "clean"? What about its temperature? Is it warm or cool to the touch? Is it wet? Dry? If you hold your stone to your cheek or forehead, what does that feel like? Does it seem like the stone is perfectly still, or does it seem like it carries a vibration? What else do you notice about the way your stone feels?

Now, bring the stone up to your nose. What does it smell like? Did you expect this, or was it a surprise? While holding the stone to your face, do you feel at all inclined to stick out your tongue and taste it? If so, feel free! Next, bring your stone up to your ear. Does it transmit a sound? Does it convey silence? What do you notice about all of these sensory findings?

Finally, hold your stone up in front of your face again with your eyes closed. Still with your eyes closed, imagine that you have no idea what it is that you are holding in your hands—that it is an object you have never seen before. Prepare to open your eyes in a moment and take in this foreign object with brand-new eyes. Give yourself a count of three, "one, two, three," and open your eyes. What do you notice about the visual experience of your stone when viewed this way?

If you are with another person who is also participating in the Pleasures of Presence, take a moment to share with each other what you noticed during the invitation. If you are alone, take a moment to ponder the experience. If it is practical, jot some notes or take the time to journal about it. The "notes" app on your smartphone can be a simple way to do this.

Worry Stone

Many people talk about leaving their worries on the trail when they go for a run. The invitation "Worry Stone" is a symbolic way to do exactly that.

Invitation: Before setting your Pleasures of Presence stone down, hold it up to your heart. Close your eyes and bring to mind a recent worry or stressor that has been weighing you down. Imagine leaving this worry with your stone so that you can feel unencumbered during your run. Take a moment to formulate your worry or stressor into words, whisper it to your stone, and carefully set your stone next to the trail in a place where you will be able to locate it as you return to the trailhead. While you run, the worry stone will hold your problem for you. When you return, you may either choose to reclaim your stressor or leave it permanently with your worry stone.

What's in Motion?

An excellent way to warm up before running is to take a few minutes to walk down the trail taking in what is visibly in motion.

Invitation: Simply walk down the trail noticing what you see that is moving. If your mind wanders, gently remind yourself to return to seeking out things that are in motion. Remember to look up, down, and into the forest or your natural surroundings to see what is in

Plant Wisdom: In the Hands of Grandmother Oak

The oak tree (*Quercus* spp.) is probably one of the most recogniz-able trees in the United States. It is reassuring to know that the leaves and acorns of all varieties of oak are edible to humans, should a person find themselves lost in the wild. The bitter taste of acorns can be reduced by soaking them in water for one to two days.

Also helpful to know is the fact that oak leaves can serve as a "spit poultice" applied to a wound to stop bleeding, or to treat a burn or poison ivy rash. Simply place some oak leaves in your mouth, chew them up to release the tannins, and apply to the wound. The inner and outer bark can also be used in this way, and can be ground into a flour and eaten.

motion. If something catches your attention that you would like to stop and watch for a while, feel free to do so. After at least ten minutes of observing what is in motion, complete the invitation and reflect upon what you noticed. Either share with another person or take a moment to journal about the experience.

INVITATIONS DURING RUNNING
Pleasures of Presence

A long run can become tedious. An effective remedy is to focus on the pleasures of the sensory experience offered by natural surroundings.

Invitation: While you are running, begin by choosing one of the five senses, such as the sense of hearing. Commit all of your awareness to your sense of hearing and notice the sounds in your midst. You may notice sounds of birds, insects, and animals. You may hear man-made sounds such as cars, trucks, tractors, trains, and airplanes. You may hear people talking and laughing. You may hear children playing. You may notice more subtle sounds, such as the sounds of wind in the leaves or a babbling brook. Whatever it is, just notice it. Attempt not to judge the sounds, especially those that are man-made. Sometimes if I am bothered by sounds of traffic, I will remind myself that I had to drive a vehicle to the trailhead. This allows a sense of acceptance and forgiveness.

You might try different types of auditory invitations while you run. You might try to notice the sounds that are farthest away and then closest to you. You might even concentrate for a while on the sound of your heart beating or the sound of your breathing. Notice the sounds of your footsteps. Are there rhythms to the sounds you are hearing?

Consider altering the sensory input to your ears. Listen to the changes that occur if you cover one ear and then the other. What do you notice if you cup your hands around your ears? What other invitations can you create that involve your sense of hearing?

I will often time myself for ten to twenty minutes, focusing on just one of the senses before switching to a different sense.

Taking in the sense of vision during a trail run may seem obvious, but how often do we really see our surroundings? While running, notice the rainbow of colors that surround you. Notice the level of light or darkness. Notice movement, notice patterns, notice shapes. Look far into the distance and look close to you. What else do you see and notice?

What do you smell while you are running? Can you discern different fragrances if you focus your attention on your sense of smell? Are you surrounded by the smells of life or the smells of death and decay . . . or both? Can you pick out fragrances from different trees and flowers? What does the surface of the trail smell like? What does the air smell like? Do you notice your own smell? If you find that this invitation is difficult, take a moment to reach down and smell some grass, a flower,

the bark of a tree, or the dirt on the trail. Then notice when and where this same smell appears as you run. Commit some time to the sense of smell, as it is so easy to overlook it in our everyday lives. Do any of the fragrances on your run evoke a memory? What else do you notice?

It is easy to focus on bodily discomfort while running, but can you refocus your awareness on body parts that are feeling capable and strong? What other sensations in the body do you notice as you run?

Are there parts of your body where you seem to be holding tension? Are your neck and facial muscles tense? How about your wrists, hands, and fingers? What happens if you actively release that tension?

Finally, notice other tactile input. What does it feel like to have the air moving over your hair and skin as you run? Is there a breeze, or is the air relatively still? Is it humid or dry? What is the temperature like? How do your clothes and shoes feel on your body? Consider a body scan from head to toe, noticing both internal and external tactile sensations.

Spend a good portion of time, such as 20 minutes, on each sense. Before you know it, you will have made it up that long, hard climb and covered more distance than you can believe.

What's in Motion?

"What's in Motion?" is a terrific invitation to use while running, just as it is useful before a run. Not only does this invitation efficiently transport forest bathers to the liminal state of consciousness, but it is helpful as a safety feature for runners.

Invitation: As you are running, pay attention to what you notice that is in motion. Do you see animals, insects, or birds? Notice the movement of the leaves on trees, the grass, and other plant material. Is there moving water nearby? Are there other humans? It is always important to be aware of your surroundings while running, so honing your ability to notice subtle motion is a potentially lifesaving skill.

Gratitude Alphabet

One of the first tricks I learned to pass the time during a long run was the "Gratitude Alphabet." Although it tends to be a little more cerebral than the sensory invitations of forest bathing, I believe it to be a quite mindful technique. I developed many, many variations on this theme, and you can too!

Invitation: Start with the letter A, and think of something or someone for which or for whom you are grateful. Go all the way through the alphabet from A to Z. If you get through the alphabet and realize you failed to name an important person or item, start back over with the letter A! Modifications of the Gratitude Alphabet might include naming things you see in nature from A to Z, body parts . . . you name it.

Running with the River

This invitation requires a trail that runs next to a body of running water, such as a river or creek, that you can run alongside of, downstream.

Invitation: As you run, notice the flow of the water. Find a floating object, like a leaf or a twig, that is next to you. Attempt to keep the item in your gaze as you run. You will lose the item as it gets pulled underwater or floats too far downstream, or as you move your eyes from trail to water and back, so simply pick another one and keep going. You may even find ripples in the water to run with. Just continue finding new focal points as they flow down the river or creek. What do you notice about *your* flow as you run with the river?

Falling Leaves

Trail running in autumn can be an emotional experience in and of itself. Making a point to notice the intricacies of falling leaves can make it even more awe-inspiring.

Invitation: During a fall trail run, look up when you are able. See if you can spot leaves just at the moment they are dropping from the branch. This may require use of the senses of vision and hearing both. Can you

catch the moment a leaf drops from a tree? How many are you able to witness? What do you notice after running like this for a while?

Nature's Hopscotch

Trail running requires a certain amount of agility to negotiate roots, rocks, and other sources of uneven terrain. Nature provides numerous opportunities to refine one's skill.

Invitation: Play a game of hopscotch, so to speak, with items on the trail. Depending upon the time of year and the species of plants and trees along your trail, start to notice the debris beneath your feet. If there is a recurring theme of debris, make it into a game. For instance, if fall leaves adorn your trail, choose a color of leaf. Decide that you are going to step on only red leaves, for example. When the options change, find a new challenge: gray rocks, perhaps. Be cautious with nuts or other rolling items that may cause you to twist an ankle, but have fun with this invitation. What do you notice? Does this remind you of anything?

Owl Eyes

Even little kids know that owls can turn their heads up to almost 270 degrees. Imagine what you could see if you had this range of motion. Even though most humans can turn their heads about 90 degrees in each direction, and have about 180 degrees in their field of vision, sometimes our ability to focus shuts out much of the available input. A standard invitation that forest therapy guides often use is "Owl Eyes." This is a great way to expand your field of vision while running on a trail.

Invitation: As you are running, raise your hands to the sides of your face. Imagine that you are creating blinders like the kind used on horses. Starting with your hands close to your eyes, notice what it is like to see only the inside of this field, without access to your peripheral vision. As you continue, attempt to soften your gaze so that you are taking in *all* the visual input within the space framed by your hands. Does it seem like your field of vision is smaller or larger than usual? Move your head side to side and up and down, taking in the entire framed field of vision. Next, move your hands outward to expand your framed field of vision. Again, work to take in the entire field of vision that is available to you. Continue on in this way for several minutes, seeing the world through owl eyes. What do you notice?

INVITATIONS AFTER RUNNING
Worry Stone

Remember that stone that held your worry while you ran? You may notice that it remains right where you left it at the trailhead. This is the moment where you have a choice to make. You may choose to pick up your stone again and reclaim your worry. On the other hand, you may choose to thank your stone and allow it to hold on to your worry forever. Either way, what do you notice about your worry after your run? What was it like to relinquish it either temporarily or permanently? Did your run provide any new insight into this problem? The forest has the tendency to be an excellent therapist.

Sit Spot

Consider taking time for Sit Spot after your run. After taking a moment to stretch, find a place to sit either on the ground or on a bench, tree trunk, or rock. Simply take in the sounds, sights, smells, and other senses of your surroundings for twenty minutes, if you are able. You may find yourself reflecting upon the sensory experiences and the medicine of the forest that you encountered during your run. You may notice plants, animals, insects, and other beings in your midst. Just take it all in and, if possible, jot your observations in a journal or sketch afterward.

TEA CEREMONY: YARROW

Yarrow tea is an appropriate post-run tea ceremony plant and is really a "top-ten plant to know" for the outdoor adventurer. See the sidebar "Nature's Ancient Remedy for Bleeding—Yarrow" for more information on this fabulous plant.

Herbal Insight: Nature's Ancient Remedy for Bleeding—Yarrow

How often, when you're running a long distance, does that ancient Greek marathon come to mind? The Battle of Marathon was fought in 490 BC with free men fighting against suppression and slavery, allowing the concept of democracy to become established. Upon winning this battle, Greek legend has it that the messenger Pheidippides ran the 26.2 miles from Marathon to Athens to share news of the victory. He collapsed and died from exhaustion, and the story became the inspiration for the marathon event, first introduced at the 1896 Olympics.

Greek mythology holds that Achilles, one of the great mythical heroes, fought in the Trojan War in about the twelfth century BC. The story goes that Achilles was a mighty, infallible warrior, but that he had one weakness: his "Achilles heel." This "Achilles heel" resulted from his mother's attempts to render him immortal by dipping him in the River Styx, whose waters were said to grant invincibility from the gods. She did so by holding baby Achilles by the heel, leaving this part of his body unanointed. Ultimately, Achilles was shot and killed by an enemy's arrow in the one place he was vulnerable, his heel.

There is also *herbal* lore surrounding the myth of Achilles. It is said that Achilles used the styptic plant yarrow to stop his soldiers' bleeding during battle. This plant, whose Latin name is *Achillea millefolium*, is therefore named in his honor. Research studying the chemical makeup of this plant has confirmed these styptic properties or, in other words, yarrow's ability to stop bleeding when applied to a wound.

The styptic properties of yarrow have secured its use for both internal and external bleeding throughout history. Dried yarrow (leaf and flower) powder can be used to stop a nosebleed, and both fresh and dried leaf and flower can be applied directly to an open wound to stop bleeding. Yarrow can also be made into an alcohol-based tincture that may be applied to injured areas.

Individuals with allergies to plants in the aster family should not consume yarrow. Although its antispasmodic properties can benefit menstrual and stomach cramps, ingesting yarrow is not recommended in early pregnancy due to this potential to relax the uterus. Yarrow has the potential to interact with blood-thinning medications due to its effect on blood clotting, and has theoretical interactions with lithium, anti-hypertensives, anticonvulsants, and sedatives if taken internally.

Using yarrow topically is generally considered safe for most individuals, so the next time you notice it alongside the trail, remember Achilles and keep this botanical warrior in mind if you happen to fall and scrape your heel.

Native to Eurasia, yarrow has been naturalized to North America and is found in all fifty states as well as throughout Canada. It has the tendency to become invasive and is often found in areas of disturbed soil, making it commonly seen on trails and at trailheads.

You will quickly learn to distinguish yarrow by its alternating rows of tiny leaves, by remembering its Latin name *millefolium*, which means, literally, "thousand leaves." Its blossoms are clusters of small white (sometimes yellow) flowers extending from the stalk in an irregular, triangular shape.

A member of the aster family, yarrow is closely related to chamomile and chrysanthemum. It typically blooms between June and September, often being found in meadows, ditches, and other dry, sunny areas.

Herbalists consider yarrow tea to be one of the most effective natural fever reducers. Fresh leaves can even be chewed to effectively relieve a toothache. Finally, one study found that *achillea* species have activity against numerous bacteria, fungi, and parasites, as well as potent anti-inflammatory abilities (Saeidnia 2011).

As you enjoy your yarrow tea, consider the rich history of the plant and its folklore. It boggles the mind to ponder some of the plants that we see on a regular basis, and just how many centuries they have inhabited this earth. Consider, too, during the tea ceremony, the animals and birds that have lived in this space for many, many years. Finally, acknowledge our human ancestors who lived in this place for generations before us. Who were they? What did they call this place? Take a moment to thank the beings in the more-than-human world and the Native people who tended this land long before we arrived.

In Closing

We run from our problems. We run away. We run ourselves ragged. We run into old friends. We get rundown. We run amok. We run out. We run. We run. We run run run run run.

As a snotty teenager, I once took out a globe, traced 180 degrees around it, and told my mother that that exact spot was where I was going to live when I grew up: as far away on the planet from my current surroundings as possible. That spot was somewhere near Christmas Island in the South Pacific. Later, in my final year of medical school, I spent ten weeks fairly close to that spot in the island nation of Vanuatu, located about halfway between Fiji and Australia, for a medical clerkship in a developing country. The work was hard, the people were amazing, the food was awful, the island was beautiful, medical advances were not available, patients thrived and patients died. I experienced my first glimpse of outdoor medicine in the open-air well-baby clinics, I became relatively proficient in the language of Bislama, and I learned to scuba dive. I learned more about medicine and humanity in those ten weeks than in my previous three and a half years of medical school combined.

The day before I left Vanuatu, I spent the afternoon sitting on a huge rock overlooking the bay on the island of Efate. I did some sketching, but I mostly just sat—"Sit Spot," it turns out. It was on that rock that I realized we cannot run from our problems, even if we run halfway around the globe. It was also on that rock that I realized there was much more to wellness and healing than Western medicine, and that *nature heals*.

IN CLOSING

The universe buries strange jewels deep within us all, and then stands back to see if we can find them.

—Elizabeth Gilbert, *Big Magic*

If someone had told me ten years ago that I would be writing a book that combines outdoor adventure, mindfulness, the practice of forest bathing, herbal medicine, conservation and environmental consciousness, and the science of nature and wellness, with sections dedicated to special populations and organizations that are offering amazing service, I would have thought they were out of their mind. My stressed-out, burned-out, exhausted, pill-prescribing, conventional-minded self would not have been able to even conceive of what half of these things even are: *forest bathing? FOREST . . . BATHING?*

Fortunately, when life leaves you crumpled in a heap as a hollowed-out shell of a being, you have the opportunity to pull yourself up by your bootstraps. When I suddenly found myself a widow, in a suffocating job that had become incongruent with every fiber of my being, I was fortunate to have the unwavering support of family, parents who picked up the pieces, a handful of forever friends, two beautiful kids, and some fabulous step-kids to stick around for.

With no idea how to go on, I followed my curiosity and I found my mentors. I was profoundly affected by author Elizabeth Gilbert's idea: "Instead of that anxiety about chasing a passion that you're not even feeling, do something that's a lot simpler, just follow your curiosity." I found that that always leads you in the right direction, as your greater Self somehow *knows.*

I spent time with the brilliantly intuitive author and healer Martha Beck, who told me to rest and play. She taught me to decipher and believe my own intuition and to follow my true life's purpose. I did deep, deep work with Nita Gage, psychologist and cofounder of the Healer Within, who taught me to tap into my subconscious and do what I came here to do. Week after week, I fought demons and unraveled my psyche with Naomi McCormick, my gifted therapist. These wise women instilled in me the notion that when you follow your own true purpose, the Universe conspires to help you.

I asked questions and questions and questions and questions. I listened and trusted the answers. I studied integrative and herbal medicine, two decisions that came from the heart with little regard for logistics. I learned herbal and life wisdom from Tieraona Low Dog, one of the world's true masters of both. Throughout it all, I ran, I biked, I paddled, I skied, I climbed, I hiked, I scuba dived, and I did yoga. I forest bathed before I knew it was called that, and I embraced it as soon as I did. I found another true mentor in Amos Clifford, whose wisdom and calling brought *shinrin-yoku* to my part of the world.

My soul searching led me to this day and the writing of this book. Were it not largely for my late husband, Dave, who on his deathbed urged me to listen to my heart, and my now husband, Joe, who is beside me every step of the way, I would still be seeing patients the same old way and chasing passions I wasn't even feeling.

It fascinated me to hear common themes among the many people I interviewed for this book. I talked to outdoor enthusiasts, nature lovers, forest therapy guides, outdoor outfitters, instructors, experts in their field, and elite athletes. Central to all of these people was a love of their sport, a need for the outdoors, a sense of both solace and wellness

when engaged in their sport, and a conviction that being outdoors was an integral component of all of it.

There was an inherent sense among these people that whether or not we can study and quantify the effects of time spent in nature, it is critical for our health and well-being. As outdoor enthusiast and certified forest therapy guide Sage Raindancer says, "Working out, training, and recreating in nature definitely has a positive effect on my mental, emotional, and (obviously) physical well-being. It's everything from feeling the spring heat and grit of a rock wall pressing into my hands as I climb; to smelling the impending summer rain as I pedal toward base camp; to feeling the pulling force of the current as I paddle upriver; to hearing the crunch of virgin snow as I clip into skis for the first run of the day. Those are the moments, where I feel that I'm 'in the zone,' that hyperawareness of being in tune with myself and my bike, skis, or kayak—it's that moment of being one with my sport at the time. It's the immersion of my senses (more than the typical five) that brings me into mindfulness when I'm physically active outside."

I must admit that hearing testimonials like this over and over and over as I compiled this work gave me a renewed sense of hope in humanity. It is not often that most people speak of these things, but when given an opportunity it seemed that, interview after interview, sentiments like this were just waiting at the tip of the tongue.

I found it heartening to see that conservation efforts were high-lighted in the missions of the organizations that govern the sports included in this book. I believe with all my heart that forest bathing is a vehicle for the advancement of environmentalism. As I often say, it is not possible to be moved by the practice of forest bathing and then proceed to damage the earth. And from my experience thus far, forest bathing is a practice that transforms even the greatest of skeptics.

An issue that will continue to challenge all forms of outdoor adventure is that of mindful trail and land use in places where some believe these types of activity should be banned. In speaking with proponents on both sides of the divide, my perspective was certainly expanded. My husband, Joe Hackenmiller, an avid mountain biker, dedicated bike commuter, bike mechanic, and certified professional mountain bike instructor, has a knack for bridging these discussions with dissenters. Interacting with birders, stargazers, hikers, horseback riders, and hunt-ers, he has a great approach. "I think it's important for us to remember that regardless of our method of outdoor recreation, we depend upon each other for a louder voice for the land," he said. "We mistakenly see each other as the enemy because we choose to enjoy public land in a different manner or by different means. It's only when we learn to work together and understand each other better that we will have a greater voice to properly save the land and become stewards. It's selfish to think that we should be able to negatively impact others with our choice of recreation. We have to work together, find a common ground, and realize that not all land is suitable for every activity and that what's right for the land should be the final deciding factor."

As we find common ground with others, we must also seek balance between the increasingly ubiquitous lure of technology and much-needed time away from it. In a book about forest bathing, one would expect a full dismissal of all things electronic; however, I think it is possible to be savvy. The preceding chapters highlighted apps and websites that today allow us to find trails and to find parks for kids to play in. We can find local forest therapy guides on an interactive map (www .natureandforesttherapy.org). We can learn the names of native lands and local plants, and about organizations for all kinds of causes. There is even a website that maps trees planted by the organization Trees Forever, in partnership with the US Forest Service, that shows a calculation of the economic benefits and environmental impacts of each tree planted (www.treesforever.org/treemap).

It is my hope that this book will bring to others even a glimpse of the joy and fulfillment that forest bathing and outdoor adventure have given me. Whether for recreation or to hone competitive skills, my wish is that it will contribute. I hope readers will take invitations from one chapter and modify them for any activity. I hope, too, that readers will invent their own invitations and applications and share them with me. I hope that the wisdom and medicine of plants, our earliest healers, will come through in this book. As Dr. Tieraona Low Dog teaches, we have coevolved with plants. There are chemicals in plants that specifically match receptors in the human body. We need each other for health and well-being, and deep, deep down, we know

this. It is also my hope that through the language of the forest, we can become kinder, gentler, and more tolerant of others, of humans who are not just like us, of the land, and of all the beings of the more-than-human world.

As I write these last words, I sit in the traditional lands of the Očeti Šakówiŋ (or Lakota Sioux), Sauk, Meskwaki, and Iowa tribes. I reflect upon and thank these people who came long before me for their stewardship of this land. With deference and gratitude to the Lakota Sioux, I offer their prayer of oneness and harmony with all forms of nature: for people, animals, birds, insects, trees and plants, rocks, rivers, mountains, and valleys, "*Mitákuye Oyás'in.*"

ACKNOWLEDGMENTS

Thank you . . .

to my teachers, mentors, and healers, Dr. Nita Gage, Dr. Martha Beck, Dr. Tieraona Low Dog, Dr. Andrew Weil, Dr. Victoria Maizes, Dr. Rubin Naiman, and Dr. Naomi McCormick, for opening my eyes to integrative medicine and the world of healing that transcends reliance upon pharmaceutical drugs.

to Mary McInnis, my teacher of yoga, fellow adventurer, ardent supporter, confidant, and sole member of my no-excuses club.

to Brock Bartholomew, Dr. Erica Smith, and Rebecca Schultze for being up for adventure and/or moral support, *always.*

to Amos Clifford for the deep wisdom of bringing forest therapy to the United States, and for ANFT teachers and mentors Caitlin Williams, Carolynne Crawley, Pamela Wirth, Nadine Mazzola, Melanie Choukas-Bradley, and Ben Page.

to Clare Kelley for being a friend, connector, and visionary; to the members of my ANFT Cohort 10; and to all of the ANFT guides around the globe who share their gifts with others.

to Florence Williams, my kindred spirit, for expanding nature consciousness through the written word.

to Christian Beckwith for shifting minds and moving mountains.

to Dr. Robert Zarr, Dr. David Sabgir, and Dr. Nooshin Razani for being my tribe of medical docs who passionately prescribe nature.

to all of the mindful adventurers who contributed to this work, sharing photos and intimate reflections that were energizing, motivating, uplifting, and inspiring.

to the insightful and altruistic founders of projects that use nature to teach, heal, transform, and save others.

to Evan Helmlinger at FalconGuides for fathoming, appreciating, and conspiring to create this work.

to, above all others, my loving family for their everlasting support: Barbara and Wallace Parrish; Steve and Kerry Parrish; my amazing kids and stepchildren, John and Elise, Nick, Kristine, Sara, Dan, Tom, Jordyn, Kimberly, Kenya, and Joey; to my late husband, Dave Bartlett, for encouraging me until the very end (and beyond); and to my husband, Joe Hackenmiller, for being by my side with endless patience, guidance, faith, and love.

to the tenders of the Earth, now and for generations before me, and to all of the beings in the more-than-human world.

Bluebell tea

APPENDIX:
HOW TO CREATE
A TEA CEREMONY

In keeping with Japanese tradition, the practice of *shinrin-yoku* typically ends with a tea ceremony. Why not conclude your mindful outdoor activity, where elements of forest bathing have been employed, with this delightful custom? People are often surprised to learn that plants within our midst can be used to create a delicious and therapeutic tea. Below are the basics for preparing your very own tea ceremony.

The first step in preparing for a tea ceremony is to confirm that foraging, or picking plants or plant parts for consumption, is allowed in the area in which you are forest bathing. In some parks, grounds, and botanical gardens, foraging is strictly prohibited. A phone call to the local parks director, ranger, or property director will answer this question. While speaking with this individual, it is also important to ask if or when any pesticides or herbicides might have been used in the area. Needless to say, foraging is not recommended where chemicals have been applied.

Secondly, it is imperative that one is able to identify potential tea plants with 100 percent accuracy. There are many similarities between various plants, and poisonous look-alikes do exist. It is always wise to double- and triple-check various resources before consuming a wild plant. Often, local naturalists will offer plant identification walks, and numerous books and online resources are available for this purpose.

One may even take a class from a local herbalist—they're out there! If there is any degree of uncertainty about foraging local plants, it is always wise to bring commercially prepared tea from home. Ideally, one would bring a dried tea from a local plant!

Once the first and second steps have been taken, the spirit of forest bathing calls for employing an ethic of tenderness, otherwise known as "wild tending." This is taught by Amos Clifford, founder of the Association of Nature and Forest Therapy, and he often refers to the book *Tending the Wild*, by M. Kat Anderson. This concept of "wild tending" holds the view of all life as being related, equal, and highly intelligent. Anderson writes that "Homo sapiens are full participants in nature, and they share mutual obligations and intricate interactions with many other forms of life." As such, in this spirit of wild tending, we show care as we forage and harvest plants, first by asking permission, secondly by offering something in return to the plant (perhaps some water, a song, and definitely a thank-you), and finally by taking only what we need and by never decimating all of the flowers or leaves of a single plant for our use.

The specifics of creating the tea are then very simple after the first three steps have been followed. Simply take a heat-tolerant vessel (a teapot, an insulated bottle, or even a large glass canning jar) and generously fill it with the plant specimen. Pour nearly boiling water over the plant, cover, and allow the tea to steep for five to ten minutes.

During a guided forest bathing walk, the guide will often use the time during steeping to share knowledge and wisdom with the group.

This may involve information about the forest, the archaeological history of the region, the ancestral history of Native tribes, or the watershed area of the trail, or it may involve information about the medicinal properties and edible uses of the tea plant. In an unguided walk, one might consider bringing a book or field guide for this steeping-time portion of the tea ceremony.

When the tea has adequately steeped, it may simply be poured off into a drinking cup. Often, if poured slowly, the plant will strain itself out from falling into the cup.

Before tasting the tea, it is traditional to pour an extra cup to offer back to the land as an act of gratitude. Finally, it is customary to culminate with one last invitation: Close your eyes and bring the tea to your nose to experience the aroma. What do you notice? And then, while remembering the way in which the forest was brought into your body through all of the other senses, invite the forest into your body, now, through your sense of taste. Bring the cup to your lips and taste the tea. What do you notice?

Enjoy as much or as little of the tea as you wish, and return the remainder to the forest, away from the trail.

The tea ceremony is often completed by inviting the participants to share one word that expresses their feelings or emotions at the end of the forest bathing practice. Why not take a moment to close your eyes, allow one word to arise, and finish your own forest bathing experience this way?

RESOURCES AND RECOMMENDED READING

Anderson, Kat. 2013. *Tending the Wild: Native American Knowledge and the Management of California's Natural Resources.* University of California Press.

Berman, Marc G., John Jonides, and Stephen Kaplan. 2008. "The Cognitive Benefits of Interacting with Nature." *Psychological Science:* 19, no. 12, 1207–12.

Bramen, Lisa. 2017. "Saving Great Rivers." *Nature Conservancy Magazine:* June 1, 2017.

Brown, Dick, Gaétan Chevalier, and Michael Hill. 2010. "Pilot Study on the Effect of Grounding on Delayed-Onset Muscle Soreness." *Journal of Alternative and Complementary Medicine:* 16(3), 265–73.

Camazine, Scott, and Robert A Bye. 1980. "A study of the medical ethnobotany of the Zuni Indians of New Mexico." *Journal of Ethnopharmacology:* 2(4):365–88.

Chevalier, Gaétan, Stephen T. Sinatra, James L. Oschman, and Richard M. Delany. 2013. "Earthing (Grounding) the Human Body Reduces Blood Viscosity—a Major Factor in Cardiovascular Disease." *Journal of Alternative and Complementary Medicine:* 19 (2): 102–10.

Choukas-Bradley, Melanie. 2018. *The Joy of Forest Bathing: Reconnect with Wild Places & Rejuvenate Your Life.* New York: Rock Point Publishing.

Clifford, M. Amos. 2013. *A Little Handbook of Shinrin-Yoku*. Santa Rosa, CA: Association of Nature and Forest Therapy.

Clifford, M. Amos. 2018. *Your Guide to Forest Bathing: Experience the Healing Power of Nature*. Newburyport, MA: Conari.

Csikszentmihalyi, Mihaly. 1990. *Flow*. New York: Harper & Row.

Ghaly, Maurice, and Dale Teplitz. 2004. "The biologic effects of grounding the human body during sleep as measured by cortisol levels and subjective reporting of sleep, pain, and stress." *Journal of Alternative and Complementary Medicine*: 10(5):767–76.

Ghorbani, Alireza, Ali Khalili, and Laleh Zamani. 2013. "The Efficacy of Stinging Nettle (Urtica Dioica) in Patients with Benign Prostatic Hyperplasia: A Randomized Double-Blind Study in 100 Patients." *Iranian Red Crescent Medical Journal*: 15(1):9–10.

Gladstar, Rosemary. 2012. *Medicinal Herbs: A Beginner's Guide*. North Adams, MA: Storey Publishing.

Han, Jin-Woo, Han Choi, Yo-Han Jeon, Chong-Hyeon Yoon, Jong-Min Woo, and Won Kim. 2016. "The Effects of Forest Therapy on Coping with Chronic Widespread Pain: Physiological and Psychological Differences between Participants in a Forest Therapy Program and a Control Group." *International Journal of Environmental Research and Public Health*: 13(3): 255.

Hartig, Terry, Marlis Mang, and Gary W. Evans. 1991. "Restorative Effects of Natural Environment Experiences." *Environment and Behavior*: 23, no. 1, 3–26.

Hartig, Terry, Gary W. Evans, Larry D. Jamner, Deborah S. Davis, and Tommy Gärling. 2003. "Tracking restoration in natural and urban field settings." *Journal of Environmental Psychology*: 23(2): 109–23.

Höld, Karen M., Nilantha S. Sirisoma, Tomoko Ikeda, Toshio Narahashi, and John E. Casida. 2000. "alpha-Thujone (the active component of absinthe): gamma-Aminobutyric acid type A

receptor modulation and metabolic detoxification." Proceedings of the National Academy of Sciences: 97(8): 3826–31.

Johnson, Rebecca, et al. 2010. *National Geographic Guide to Medicinal Herbs: The World's Most Effective Healing Plants*. Washington, DC: National Geographic Society.

Kabat-Zinn, Jon. 2018. "A Guided Walking Meditation to Savor Fall." Mindful (website). September 27, 2018.

Li, Qing. 2018. *Forest Bathing: How Trees Can Help You Find Health and Happiness*. New York: Viking.

Li, Qing, K. Morimoto, M. Kobayashi, H. Inagaki, M. Katsumata, Y. Hirata, K. Hirata, et al. 2008. "Visiting a Forest, but Not a City, Increases Human Natural Killer Activity and Expression of Anti-Cancer Proteins." *International Journal of Immunopathology and Pharmacology*: 21(1): 117–27.

Matthews, Dorothy M., and Susan M. Jenks. 2013. "Ingestion of Mycobacterium vaccae decreases anxiety-related behavior and improves learning in mice." *Behavioural Processes*: vol. 96: 27–35.

Miyazaki, Yoshifumi. 2018. *Shinrin Yoku: The Japanese Art of Forest Bathing*. Portland, OR: Timber Press.

Morita E, S. Fukuda, J. Nagano, N. Hamajima, H. Yamamoto, Y. Iwai, T. Nakashima, H. Ohira, and T. Shirakawa. 2007. "Psychological effects of forest environments on healthy adults: Shinrin-yoku (forest-air bathing, walking) as a possible method of stress reduction." *Public Health*: 121(1):54–63.

Razani, Nooshin, Saam Morshed, Michael A. Kohn, Nancy M. Wells, Doug Thompson, Maoya Alqassari, Amaka Agodi, and George W. Rutherford. 2018. "Effect of park prescriptions with and without group visits to parks on stress reduction in low-income parents: SHINE randomized trial." *PLoS One*.

Rose, Lisa. 2017. *Midwest Medicinal Plants*. Portland, OR: Timber Press.

Saeidnia, S., A. Gohari, N. Mokhber-Dezfuli, and F. Kiuchi. 2011. "A review on phytochemistry and medicinal properties of the genus Achillea." *Daru: Journal of Faculty of Pharmacy*, Tehran University of Medical Sciences: 19(3): 173–86.

Vigsø, Bent, and Vita Nielsen. 2006. *Børn & udeliv* [Children and Outdoor Activity]. Esbjerg: CVU Vest Press.

Whiteley, Sharon, and Ann Marie Chiasson. 2018. *Barefoot Wisdom: Better Health through Grounding*. Atglen, PA: Schiffer.

Williams, Florence. 2017. *The Nature Fix*. New York: W.W. Norton.

PHOTO CREDITS

I would like to extend my sincere gratitude and appreciation to all the photographers and their subjects who captured and shared their outdoor adventures in the inspiring and breathtaking images contained in this book.

—*Suzanne Bartlett Hackenmiller*

aimintang/Getty Images: 36

Angel Johnston: iii, x, 205, 206, 209

Azure-Dragon/Getty Images: 162, 163

Callie Lipkin: 216, 217, 218, 228

Darrin Siefkin: xiii, xxv, 2, 5, 8, 22, 27, 42, 48, 58, 62, 66, 69, 138, 155

David Sharratt: 108

DmitriyKazitsyn/Getty Images: 161

Erica Smith: iv, xiv, 13, 14, 113, 118, 125, 142

Erick Schrier: xv, 38, 167, 226

Fabio Ticozzi/Getty Images: 122

Holly Truitt: 105

Iuliia Morozova/Getty Images: 163

Ivan Marjanovic/Getty Images: 71

Jessica Cruz: 173, 178, 180, 185, 186, 189, 190, 192, 194, 200

Joe Hackenmiller: 33, 100, 134, 149

Kip Ladage: 199

krblokhin/Getty Images: 65

Kristin Cleveland: viii, 6, 80, 156

makasana/Getty Images: 183

Melanie Drake: 145, 164

ngoodman/Getty Images: 31

orzeczenie/Getty Images: 197

osoznaniejizni/Getty Images: 133

Photitos2016/Getty Images: 183

portgrimes/Getty Images: 115

rannica/Getty Images: 103

Rebecca Schultze: vii, 168

Svetlana Popova/Getty Images: 198

Tara Sundt: 45

Wendy Foote: 11

Yevgeniy Drobotenko/Getty Images: 162

ABOUT THE AUTHOR

Suzanne Bartlett Hackenmiller, MD, is an OB-GYN and Integrative Medicine physician who currently lives and practices in Iowa. She completed OB-GYN residency at Western Pennsylvania–Temple University in Pittsburgh and is a fellowship graduate of the University of Arizona Center for Integrative Medicine. She is board certified by both the American Board of Obstetrics and Gynecology and the American Board of Integrative Medicine. She holds additional certifications in herbal medicine and is a certified forest therapy guide. She currently serves as medical director for the Association of Nature and Forest Therapy.

Dr. Bartlett Hackenmiller's interest in integrative medicine and nature therapy arose from her personal journey through raising a child on the autism spectrum, her late husband's death from cancer, dealing with physician burnout, the inadequacies of conventional medicine, and her personal discovery of wellness and solace in both outdoor adventure and mindfulness in nature. She and her current husband, Joe, share a passion for leading workshops combining outdoor adventure and the practice of *shinrin-yoku*/Japanese forest bathing for women's empowerment, individuals with special needs, cancer survivors, veterans, and others.

She is the author of an award-winning children's book, *A Friend Like John: Understanding Autism*, and speaks nationally and internationally on the subject of autism, integrative medicine, and nature therapy.

More information is available at her website, www.Integrative Initiative.com.